SOULBRIETY

SOULBRIETY

A Plan to Heal Your Trauma, Overcome
Addiction, and Reconnect with Your Soul

ELISA HALLERMAN, PhD

hachette
BOOKS

NEW YORK

Copyright © 2022 by Elisa Hallerman
Cover design by Sara Pinsonault
Cover copyright © 2022 by Hachette Book Group, Inc.

Hachette Go, an imprint of Hachette Books
Hachette Book Group
1290 Avenue of the Americas
New York, NY 10104
HachetteGo.com
Facebook.com/HachetteGo
Instagram.com/HachetteGo

First Edition: December 2022

Hachette Books is a division of Hachette Book Group, Inc.

The Hachette Go and Hachette Books name and logos are trademarks of Hachette Book Group, Inc.

The publisher is not responsible for websites (or their content) that are not owned by the publisher.

Print book interior design by Linda Mark.

Library of Congress Cataloging-in-Publication Data

Names: Hallerman, Elisa, author.
Title: Soulbriety : a plan to heal your trauma, overcome addiction, and
    reconnect with your soul / Elisa Hallerman, PhD.
Description: First edition. | New York : Hachette Go, [2022] |
    Includes bibliographical references.
Identifiers: LCCN 2022019083 | ISBN 9780306827723 (hardcover) |
    ISBN 9780306827747 (ebook)
Subjects: LCSH: Soul—Psychological aspects. | Self-perception. |
    Addicts—Rehabilitation. | Healing—Psychological aspects.
Classification: LCC BF697.5.S43 H355 2022 | DDC 158.1—dc23/eng/20220729
LC record available at https://lccn.loc.gov/2022019083

ISBNs: 9780306827723 (hardcover), 9780306827747 (ebook)

Printed in Canada

MRQ-T

10 9 8 7 6 5 4 3 2 1

For those still suffering from the disease of addiction,
and for those who have lost loved ones to its cunning grasp.
May you constantly be guided by soul.

Contents

Foreword

'm at the age where looking at my life, my only real regret
is the time wasted, spent on trivial pursuits. The proverbial
rabbit hole we *all* go down, whether or not our name is Alice.
We all chase the same externals—the digital validation—and
since none of us are immune from life on life's often harsh
terms we *all* tumble into the labyrinth of the deadly diptych
of delusion and denial that can keep us in this perpetual spin
cycle.

In this time of global crisis and climate catastrophe there
is always hope, a steady pulse of seeking. Seeking answers.
Seeking connection. Seeking love. With all the filtered external reminders, particularly through the devices that we carry
with and on us at all times, what I have learned and have been
helped by Dr. Elisa Hallerman to learn is that, in the end, it's
about our SOUL.

I believe that when you're looking in the mirror, you're
looking at the problem, and many of us need guides to help

clear away the noise and shrapnel of our ancestral imprints and access that beautiful centerpoint that is our essential self inside its womb that carries and nurtures us, our SOUL.

What impresses me about Dr. Hallerman's book is her unflinching and raw storytelling and experience, strength and hope honed by her deep seeking and learning. The overall message is that we *are* enough, but every day we *can* do something to deepen our connection with our own SOULBRIETY.

I remember the day she told me that that was the title of her book, and I cried because it hit at my center. That my recovery from drugs and alcohol addiction weren't enough. It needed to be deeper work.

Now, I have the privilege of undergoing psychoanalysis, and that has helped me profoundly, but obviously many, many people do not. A book like this can shift you into a new gear, a new level of self-understanding and, most importantly, self-love.

I have recommended countless people to consult with Dr. Hallerman, and I recommend this book with that same fervor. It is an important work, from a special, learned professional whose own SOULBRIETY comes at a crucial time for us all.

Jamie Lee Curtis

Introduction

I'm alone, in the back of a taxi headed to Benny's apartment. It's midnight, but he is expecting me. I made an appointment. By "appointment" I mean I called him obsessively until he woke up and agreed I could come over. I ask the cab to wait; I just have to run in and grab something. Benny's door is open and I walk in. As always, the one-room apartment is dark and smoky, with that weird kitchen smell of garlic and spices. I sit on the bed, not even aware of how gross that is. The bed that seems to take up the whole apartment. Benny is dressed in a black robe and he looks seventy years old and I wonder how long he's been doing this. He walks into a tiny alcove on the other side of the room and puts my baggies together. Carefully—by which I mean painfully slowly—measuring a gram per bag. I'm buying three grams, each in its own baggie. We both know I might as well get an eight ball, which is one large bag with just half a gram more than I'm buying. But for some reason, needing that much makes me feel ashamed. It feels like too much to do alone. In my mind, it's reserved only for a group event. Not that I'm doing parties anymore—those days are over. Though I don't admit it to myself, I'm too sick for that. I just want to be alone. I won't even use at home anymore; I can't bear the shame. This is a one-woman party, just me and a hotel room and the only thing I care about anymore. A handful of gram baggies it is.

"I need something now," I say. Benny ignores me. It feels like it is taking hours to get my tiny packages ready and my body is screaming for it. After an eternity, he finally turns around and I push the cash into his hand. He slowly turns over the coke and says goodnight. But I'm not leaving yet. Like a woman who hasn't seen her lover in a year, I ravenously open one of the baggies, pour the white powder on the countertop and do a line. Right there in his disgusting, dirty kitchen. Who knows what's been on that countertop, how many other addicts have been in there doing the same thing just tonight. But none of that matters.

Relief. Imagine being held underwater, holding your breath and not knowing when or if you'll be released. Every alarm bell going off in your body, the struggle and the panic and the fear. Then, with the touch of a button, you're released. You rise to the surface and gasp. The first line of coke is that first lungful of air: salvation mixed with gratification. My dopamine level skyrockets and everything feels like pleasure; the adrenaline kicks in and I become superhuman: superior, worthier, and more desirable.

Five minutes later, I'm back in the taxi, and the high is starting to dissipate. More coke will bring the feeling back, and it feels like I must continue or I will die. I need another bump. Like, *now.* The ride to the hotel seems endless. Should I risk it? I decide not to. I try to look composed as I walk into the hotel and up to the reception desk. My body is lit with excitement and shame at the same time. I ask for a room and she hands me my key. Does she know what I'm doing here? Does she even care? What *am* I doing here? I could just as soon have asked the taxi to take me back to my townhouse in Beverly Hills. To my kind and empathetic roommate, who somehow never judges me. But no. My room, and particularly my bed, is the one place in the world I feel safe. I never want to jeopardize that feeling by using at home.

The one question I am not asking myself is *why.* Why am I hiding away all weekend using drugs and alcohol—all alone? But looking at myself is not why I'm at this hotel. I'm here to quiet the noise in my head and ease the torment in my body. Torment that ratchets up second by second as the receptionist types my name and credit card number into the computer in what feels, to me, like slow motion.

Finally I'm in the elevator. I fumble in my purse for the bag. I use the key card the receptionist gave me, dipping the corner into the white powder and snorting another bump. Ah . . . *relief.* I do it again. And again. I forget to leave the elevator when it opens on my floor, letting the doors close again. I'm starting to relax. A minute later I hit the "door open" button and find my way to the room.

Inside, the first thing I do is lock the door. Then the dead bolt. I sit down on the floor in front of the couch and put all my baggies on the coffee table. I pour the first one out and use my credit card to chop it up; then I crush the bigger pieces down to nice fine powder. I take a dollar bill, roll it up, and snort the whole line. I think, *You really shouldn't use dollars, they are so dirty . . . that's how you get hepatitis C.* I make a mental note to order straws from room service. *Room service . . .* I crawl to the desk and pick up the phone. I think about who else might have used the phone before me, putting their sweaty face and crusty nose on the receiver. But I don't really care. I dial the phone.

"Hi, um, yeah, some friends and I are hanging out in room 306," I overexplain. "So, um, I'd like to order six beers, a bottle of vodka, a bottle of champagne, and—yeah, something to mix the vodka with, like maybe cranberry juice? Okay, great, thank you." Then I add, for effect, "Everyone will love this."

I wonder if he knows there is no "everyone." That there is only me. With all the cocaine, I'm pretty jacked up by the time the alcohol arrives. They knock but I don't want them to see me. Through the door I tell the guy to just leave it outside. Only when I am sure he is gone do I slowly open the door and pull the cart full of alcohol in the room.

Suddenly I miss my friends and family. I wish they knew my secret and would come save me. Just then my cellphone phone buzzes—a dreadful noise indicating someone is actually trying to get in touch with me. I recoil into a ball on the bed. I don't want anyone to see me in this much pain. Even having the phone in the same room makes me feel too vulnerable, so I take it to the bathroom where I wrap it in a washcloth and leave it on the sink. I return to the coffee table for comfort: another line followed by a drink. I can breathe again, if only for a moment.

The paranoia comes on slowly, a few hours in. *They are coming to get me. I'm not safe. They will take my drugs and lock me up.* Soon it becomes a frenzy. Suddenly I am moving the furniture—the overstuffed chair, the coffee table, the floor lamp—against the door. To keep *them* out. Because they are definitely coming for me. They know I'm here. I scramble up the pile to look out the peephole, then climb back down. I do it over and over, obsessively, for the hours that follow. *I have to know when they get here.*

More time . . . more coke . . . more alcohol. I realize I've made a huge mistake. I pick up the sticky room phone again and call down to the front desk. *You have to change the name on my reservation.* I give the receptionist an alias, a random combination of a first and last name I find by flipping through the hotel magazine there by the phone. She says okay and we hang up. I'm safe for the moment. But an hour later, the paranoia is getting worse. I remember thinking about calling the front desk to change my name—but did I actually do it? I can't remember, and I can't take any chances. So I pick up the phone again. This time the receptionist asks me, *Is everything okay?*

Shit, I think, *she is on to me now. I need to throw her off.*

"Yes, I'm fine," I assure her, trying to sound professional and not wasted. "It's just that my boyfriend—I mean, my ex-boyfriend actually—is looking for me, and I'm scared he will find me. But otherwise, you know, I'm good. I'm going to bed soon. Thanks so much."

"Okay," she says. I can tell she's still suspicious. "Remember, we are only a phone call away down here. Would you like me to put a Do Not Disturb on your phone?"

"Perfect," I say. "Thank you."

We hang up, and I'm immediately on my knees doing another line on the coffee table.

A while later I walk into the bathroom and catch a glimpse of myself in the mirror. I have the strangest experience of having absolutely no idea who is looking back at me. I know that person is supposed to be me, but I don't recognize her. Those are not my eyes. Looking back at me is a girl who is suffering, troubled, heartbroken. Her eyes tell a story of anguish and fear. She is not me. But if not, then who is she? And who am I, the one who is witnessing her?

Someone come save me, please. Anyone. Please.

I turn on the shower. It's my ritual at the hotel, on these solitary weekends, when I start to think too much. I try to wash off the twin stains of shame and remorse. It does not work. It never does. I towel off, put on the complimentary robe, come back out of the bathroom—and start the cycle again.

Hours roll by. Coke, alcohol, bathroom, climb up the furniture, peek through the curtains. It is endless, and it has only begun. I will be here for the next two days. This is how I will spend my weekend. Outwardly worrying that *they* are coming—while inwardly, even secretly, wishing that *someone, anyone* would show up. Anyone, to save me from the demons inside my own mind. But Sunday night, I will return to my house—alone. And Monday morning I will get up for work. I will go to the kitchen and get a bottle of beer from the fridge to help me come down from the weekend. And I will watch myself as I blow my hair dry, beer in hand, turning back into Lisa Hallerman, the young agent from United Talent Agency. An hour later, I'm sitting in the back of the conference room during our morning staff meeting with the entire company. I have a tissue in my hand because my nose is running, and I worry my sniffles are as loud as I think they are. *Someone's going to know.* I glance around to see if anyone is looking at me, feeling a familiar paranoia setting in. I focus on my breathing and try to calm down. I look down and see I am almost finished with the large cup of coffee in my hand. Coffee is my Monday-after lifeline, and I'm not going to make it through this meeting without it. So I try to ration it with smaller sips. Finally the meeting is over, and I leave with the herd of people and head straight to the kitchen to refill my cup before returning to my office to face the day.

=

EIGHT YEARS LATER, I wake up at age thirty-nine and realize it's my five-year sobriety birthday. Meaning I've been sober from drugs and alcohol for five consecutive years, which is a huge milestone in the life of any addict. I wish I could say the weekend in the hotel room was the last time I did that. It wasn't. It would take me several more years before I went to Alcoholics Anonymous and heard other women share about their years in sobriety. Having one year clean, let alone *five* years, seemed an insurmountable feat at the time. But I like to win, and that's kept me going. (There are very few upsides to being driven by an out-of-control ego and a wounded inner child, but this is one of them.) Thanks to this same tenacity, I've been able to build a name for myself in the entertainment industry as a Hollywood talent agent. I have the life I'd always envisioned for myself. In every classic sense of the term, I've "made it."

As I pull the heavy gray drapes from the French doors in my bedroom, I can hear baby birds chirping in a nest just outside. The groundskeeper was just here yesterday, so the lawn looks flawless, and the sun is shining outrageously as it only does in Southern California. Everything is exactly as I've always dreamed it would be.

And yet standing here, I feel a familiar gnawing sense of depression and despair.

I'd spent my entire time in sobriety checking off all the boxes of "success." Dream job, check. Own my own home, check. Drive my favorite car, check. Reach social butterfly status, check. Money in the bank, check. *I've already done everything I'm supposed to do*, I conclude. *Shouldn't these feelings be fixed?* I thought sobriety meant the promise of a better life and dreams coming true. Sure, I heard people mention you still have to deal with "life on life's terms," but so far nothing had seemed particularly difficult compared to the chaos of using. But here in the middle of my perfect life, on a day where I should be feeling nothing but joy, I can't help but notice that things are not at all *fixed*. Am I happy? Sure. I mean, kind of. But do I live in joy? No. Am I living in meaning and purpose? No. Have I been able to let go of the disappointments, the roadblocks, and the trauma from my past? No.

I make my morning coffee while the dogs run in the yard. Then I sit on the patio and pick up my phone to find a flurry of congratulatory messages from my family, best friends, and college roommates. They're proud of me for my sobriety, but also for everything that's happened in my career since then. As I read over the accomplishments they're naming, I don't feel proud—I feel numb. I'm aware of a deep void I'm feeling inside, and I start to cry. I know it's a big deal to get sober, and on the outside it looks like everything has gotten *way* better in my life since then. But the secret truth is that I still feel a lot

8

like that woman from five years ago on the inside. Suddenly I can't help but see what I've been unwilling to look at for years: I've traded my addiction to drugs and alcohol for an addiction to money, power, and prestige. I've been using my material success to skirt the same emptiness I'd once sought to fill through drugs and alcohol. I am still on the merry-go-round of disconnection, and it's going strong. If I don't find my way back to myself, I am destined to a lifetime of trying to fill that void.

I know I only have two choices. Either I find out what's *supposed* to fill that void, getting curious as to why it's here and what it's trying to tell me, or I stay in an addict mindset for the rest of my life: chasing the carrot of external validation and outer success to avoid looking at what's really driving me underneath.

I know what I have to do, but how on earth do I do it?

⸻

BEFORE I WAS sober from drugs and alcohol, I never gave much thought to the existence of anything beyond what I could see with my eyes. While my family was culturally Jewish, spirituality was not a part of our daily lives. As a political science and sociology major in college, and then an attorney, my belief system was anchored in the restricted realm of reason. I pretty much hung out in the external world, pulled here and there by my ego and the things that happened to me. As a result, I was easily unmoored by life's twists and turns—first using drugs and alcohol to try and keep my head above water, and later moving on to career success and material wealth.

But something happened the morning of my five-year sobriety date. I admitted to myself for the first time that my
heart was still injured and depression had never stopped hov-
ering. I wanted to know why, despite my best attempts to get
over my problems, I didn't feel better. I had to admit that I
needed a better way. The answer—which I wouldn't discover
for a few more years—was to find and reconnect with my soul.

But I couldn't have seen that at the time. Just like so many
of us in Western culture today, I was looking for an easy way
to fix myself—as quickly as possible, thanks. I was willing
to do whatever was needed to get back into action, back into
happiness mode, and back to "normal"—which for me, meant
abstinence from mind-altering substances. While science
has indeed been able to help us understand and treat certain
types of physical and mental suffering, it doesn't work when
it comes to the suffering that arises from the unconscious.
The questions I needed to be asking were about things I
couldn't see. What's underneath my addiction, depression,
and anxiety? What I didn't know then, but thankfully know
deeply today, is that these are not just any old questions.
These questions are the gateway to an infinite well of knowledge, power, and wisdom, waiting for each of us just below
the surface. These questions are the gateway to learning the
language of soul.

What do I mean when I say "soul"? It's hard to define with
words alone because soul is not a thing. You can't put your
arms around it, and you can't point to it. It's simply the essence of your being, the map of your potential, the clues on
the treasure hunt toward your purpose and destiny. We don't
have a soul; we *are* soul. Soul is absolute, certain, and genuine.

It requires care and curiosity. It is the part of us that deeply attaches to others. It's what feels like home, peace, and unity. Wholeness. Enrichment. Intimacy. Imagine a bottomless ocean teeming with life that's tailored exactly to *who you are*. That indescribable, individualized, boundless well of infinite resources is *soul*.

But if you can't describe it, how in the world are you supposed to locate it? You must listen and feel. Soul speaks when our conscious and unconscious minds are in communication, making what was previously unknown known. Soul's language is ancient, and meaningful. And it requires a deeper listening than most of us have learned.

In opposition to the incessant demand on modern humans to grow *up*, soul's nature is to grow *down*, like the roots of a tree. To fully unfurl underground, drawing from the mystery below the nourishment we need to fully expand above. But for many of us—I might say most of us—the growing down of our soul has been interrupted. Maybe once, but more often many times, in small or big ways. Something happened a long time ago that we were too young, or too afraid, to process. And out of protection, our roots had to recoil, break apart, and withdraw. The space that was left feels like a gaping wound.

As with any vacuum, there is a driving need to fill the hole. What we fill it with depends on who we are, and maybe even on how our brains are wired. What I know for sure is that people like me fill it with the high. Early on, I looked for anything that would numb the pain and provide a temporary reward or emotional boost. I covered the pain with alcohol; I tried to stuff it down with drugs. I bought things, engaged in risky and compulsive behaviors, and took part in any number of maladaptive coping strategies. The reason I kept doing it was that it *worked*—at least for a period of time. Turns out every coping mechanism has an expiration date; they may work for months or years or even decades, but they don't work forever. And when the bill comes, it is more expensive and crushing than we could have imagined.

But even after I finally woke up and got sober, the pain was still there and it still needed to be managed. So I replaced using drugs with misguided love, shiny new toys, material objects, titles and other trophies—anything to bolster my anemic sense of self. I had no idea who my "self" really was. Abstinence from drugs and alcohol had given me clarity; so-briety had given me a design for living a life that kept me *alive*. But I had yet to understand the source of my ailment. I didn't realize that there was a part of me that craved beauty and darkness, that needed to tune into my deeper longings—rather than fill the void—in order to have a creative, inspired, and desirable life. The morning of my five-year sobriety birth-day was the beginning of a new leg of that journey. I knew something had to change, and that something was *me*.

＝

IN THE YEARS since, I've left Hollywood, gotten my Ph.D. in somatic depth psychology—which is the study of bringing unconscious psychological material into the light of aware-ness through meditation, dreamwork, the study of images and archetypes, inspired by the work of Carl Jung—and started the world's first recovery management agency. I've also come to see that all the times I felt stuck, lost, scared, disconnected, uncertain, and alone were really just messages for me to pay attention. They were my deeper self urging me to get curious about *why* things were as they were, urging me to turn inward and look at the source of my pain, fear, insecurities, and feelings of emptiness. It took me several more years and a bunch of big mistakes before I discovered that the discomfort and anxiety I was trying to stuff down was the result of a disconnect from my own soul. Depth psychologists call it "soul loss"—and most of us struggle with it to some degree. Not taught to have a strong connection to our own inner guidance, we feel an incredible and fundamental longing for something we can't quite name. As a result, we try to fill the void—with food, sex, overspending, self-harm, workaholism, drugs and alcohol, ego inflation, codependency, or any of a thousand other sources of gratification. Regardless of its form, addiction is an attempt to avoid the pain that comes when we are out of sync with our source. It's an attempt to distance ourselves from the painful throb of emptiness where our soul connection should be.

What if, instead of looking for coping strategies, we reconnected to our soul as if our lives depended on it? What if we made it our top priority to stay connected, to draw inspiration and creativity from within, to allow it to guide us back to our authenticity? This is the role soul is meant to play in our lives, and in the months that followed my five-year sobriety date, I started to treat it that way. I didn't realize it at the time—I didn't really understand what the word "soul" meant yet—but somehow I made the decision to follow my own inner guidance in spite of my fear, anxiety, ego, and pride. In the process,

I began to walk a path I've since described as *Soulbriety*—a soul-centered path of recovery from addiction through healing its underlying origin: trauma.

Soul loss happens because *something happened.* Something too big and terrifying for our nervous system to process fully. In other words, it is the result of unhealed trauma. Trauma as I define it is an event or series of events that are life threatening or *feel* as if they are. The experience is too overwhelming for the individual's nervous system, sending the body into a fight-or-flight state. Traumatic experiences include the obvious: accidents, losses, divorce, illness, violence, abuse. But you might be surprised about how significantly even so-called minor trauma can impact our lives—a subject I'll go into. For now, suffice it to say that some traumatic events and experiences cannot simply be left in the past. Like it or not, the energy, feeling, and emotions continue to haunt us in the present. They drive a wedge between us and our soul, one that doesn't just go away on its own. If left unacknowledged, they can wreak havoc on our relationships, careers, and sense of self. Without a conscious intention to uncover, recognize, grieve, and heal, we will constantly be looking for something—anything—to ease the misery.

Enter addiction. Trauma leaves us with unbearable emotions, and in the beginning, addiction feels like an answer. In our drug of choice we seek the feelings of love and belonging we needed back then, when the traumatic events happened. These are innate human desires that were not, for any number of reasons, met, and some part of us is still looking to get these needs addressed. Our medicine of choice—be it drugs, alcohol, food, gambling, or shopping—helps us escape the nearly insurmountable pain. At the time, it feels like the only solution. Unfortunately, at some point down the road we realize this solution is short-lived, that the very medicine we've chosen is a poison of its own.

The only true cure for the unhealed trauma that fuels addiction is to dive more fully into our inner lives. Recovery that does not deeply reflect on our personal history, looking for and actively healing our trauma, simply passes the baton to the next coping mechanism, leaving us with more or different symptoms of addiction. That's where Soulbriety comes in.

—

FOR SO MANY years I longed for a hero to come save me—a lifelong wish, born of events that took place decades earlier. Only later did I realize that what I was truly looking for was not an external hero—what I sought had been deep inside of me all along. I was looking for my own soul. Helping others find their way back to soul is what Soulbriety is all about.

The Soulbriety approach we use at Recovery Management Agency is different from the work of an interventionist or case manager because we are not solely looking to treat the client's symptoms. Our assessments are looking for patterns: soul loss, trauma, and the effects these have on the body and the brain. We pan out from the addict themselves, to include the entire family system that birthed and informed them—and the wounds each member of that system needs to heal. This results in a more integrative approach to healing and makes the RMA team "recovery managers," not just "case managers": we are educators, advocates, and ongoing health and wellness managers for our clients. It's a lot to oversee a team of doctors, clinicians, and lawyers and keep everyone rowing the boat in the same direction, but it's worth it.

So I spend a lot of time walking my clients back from the edges where addiction has pushed them, but once that phase is past, my job is to help them heal the deeper soul loss that caused the crisis in the first place. I craft an individualized Soulbriety Plan for each client, including plans for abstinence, trauma healing, and soul recovery. Guidance in reconnecting to my soul is what I didn't have when I was coming out of my addiction, and it's why in spite of getting sober I was still so unhappy for so many years. Soulbriety fills a gaping hole in the common understanding of addiction recovery, and it's the reason treatment counselors and psychiatrists and recovery specialists watch me work and say, "Wow, I didn't even know someone like you existed." Because it's one thing to help an addict turn away from drugs and alcohol. It's another thing to turn them around and walk them back *toward* something: the essence of who they are.

Since every soul is completely unique, Soulbriety is not a one-size-fits-all methodology. It's an *approach* to recovery more than a step-by-step process, and it's applied to each person based on their unique individual needs and story. That said, there are three basic tenets that underlie the approach. First, soul is our most trustworthy guide, the deepest essence of who we are. Second, when we experience soul loss through trauma, many of us try to fill that hole and dampen the pain with addiction. Third, soul recovery requires acknowledging the trauma and healing the soul wounds themselves.

Since being a human being involves traumas of all sizes, the Soulbriety journey doesn't end with abstinence from drugs and alcohol. It continues throughout the course of your life. The endgame is for soul to be calling the shots, no matter what. Once you've started listening for the voice of soul, its volume gets turned up. You start to hear more and more clearly where soul is guiding you. (If not, trust me, the whispers get louder and louder.) While following its direction is not always easy, the benefits are worth it. Soul is with us through ups and downs, scary moments, challenges, and adversity. But only through this journey do we find the way to our core. In our most vulnerable moments, when we want to give up, when we are broken, when we are saddled with more heartache than we can bear—only then do we grow down, understand who we really are, and see what we are made of. With soul guiding us, we are incredibly strong and powerful. This power, this passion, this newfound meaning will allow us to accomplish things beyond our wildest imaginings, and our example will give others permission to do the same.

Since the journey to soul healing is unique to who each of us are, I cannot write a typical how-to book about Soulbriety. I'm not offering you a step-by-step guide for how to be abstinent from drugs and alcohol, as there are many programs out there that do that part well. This book is about the part that's missing in traditional recovery: how to make meaning of your addiction, shine a light on the soul journey you've been walking (whether you knew it or not), and heal your way back to who you really are. So it's written in soul's own language, which has nothing to do with step-by-step processes or to-do lists. Soul speaks in metaphor, symbol, and myth. In other words, *story.*

Storytelling is how we convey the things that are impossible, really, to say. This is why I ask my clients, before everything else, to tell me their story. Not what's happening right now with their addiction, but first what the story of their life is—told from the beginning, the way they experienced it. I am interested in how they see the world around them, their relationships, their families, what actions and behaviors motivate them, what they love about their lives, and how they deal with suffering. I am looking for the material that sits below their conscious awareness, rooted in the depth of their soul—a place most of them have yet to consider. I am curious about when things broke; when their soul fragmented and withdrew from their awareness. Only when I know the story can I begin to identify the trauma hidden beneath the surface. Slowly I begin to see and understand how their addiction was born and what their soul is crying out to heal. So this book is full of stories; it's built on them. The stories of my clients, and also my own story. In many ways it is my soul biography—the story of my personal soul journey: my wounds, my shame, my trauma, and my innermost vulnerabilities. I share all of these things because I know that, for you to heal your own soul loss, you'll have to excavate the same from your life. My story is also the origin story of Soulbriety itself. So think of this as a love letter from my soul to yours, and an invitation to dive into your own history. For everything you need to know is right there inside of you. You only need to be willing to look.

THE CHAPTERS THAT follow are meant to walk you through common experiences on the soul journey as they happened to me and my clients. Please note that I've organized the book in the order of my own soul journey to date. Your story, like those of my clients woven throughout, will be uniquely yours. (Speaking of which, all of the clients I mention in this book are fictionalized composites of past clientele, and many of the names and identifying characteristics of people in my life have been changed.) Soulbriety is not just about healing; it's about building resilience. I want you to live a life where, despite the hard times, you do not have to wait to feel joy. Together, we're about to embark on the most important mission of your life: a return to the essence of who you are. I am not going to suggest this is an easy path. But even with—and in some ways, because of—all its difficulties and challenges, life can be rich, full, and purposeful. Once I figured that out, my life got bigger beyond my wildest dreams. And with that in mind, sit back, get comfortable, take it slow, and let me tell you the story of soul.

AUTHOR'S NOTE: If you have not yet looked at and worked on your trauma in a clinical setting, please seek out a professional trauma practitioner or therapist to assist you. Stabilization from past trauma requires a careful hand and a loving, qualified container. Create this solid foundation for yourself and then come back to Soulbriety. It will be here waiting for you.

CHAPTER ONE

The Language of Soul

It's 11 p.m., and I'm getting ready to go to bed. It's been a really long couple of days. Mom has been in LA for the past week, and I've been taking care of her. I had to bring her here from Connecticut after she fell and broke her hip on her way home from having spine surgery. Now after two major reconstructive operations, she is in my guest room recuperating. I've fed her dinner, which is a big deal since the only thing I can cook is burned vegetables or some sort of toasted bread product, buttered or with some melted cheese if I'm feeling fancy. So there she is, in her pajamas, watching *Law & Order*. And here I am, physically drained and emotionally spent.

And then, the phone rings.

My heart drops. It's late, meaning it can be only two things. Either someone is in the hospital, or someone is in trouble. Or both. Years ago, when I was working in Hollywood, those late-night calls meant there was a problem on set, or they

21

didn't approve of the script pages for tomorrow, or they just needed a confidante they could be vulnerable with about their fears and insecurities at that exact minute, usually around 10 p.m. But now the stakes were different.

When I pick up, my client Billy's mom and dad are both on the line. His mom has just received a call from Billy's friend Jane. Jane told them Billy had been using drugs for the past couple of nights, and she was really worried about him. I've been working with Billy and his family for a few years, but this particular time, something feels different. I've known for a while that there's more going on than just the addiction to drugs. You see, people don't continue to relapse because they *want* to be a drug addict. I've never met anyone for whom that is the case. They relapse because of what lies underneath the addiction. What I call the *what* and the *why*: *what* they are running away from; *why* they are willing to destroy themselves. And the answer to the questions *what* and *why*, more often than not, is trauma.

Trauma happens when, due to unexpected or painful events, our nervous system is overwhelmed beyond its capacity to process the experience in real time. It can be acute, chronic, or complex. It might be caused by a one-time event or a series of events. It might simply be the result of the environment in which you were raised. In a nutshell, trauma is *any experience that takes us out of the window of our tolerance.* When something happens that is unknown or overwhelming, our brain cannot make sense of it. In an effort to dampen the intensity, our processing slows down—which is why sometimes it feels like traumatic events are happening in slow motion. Our brains cannot properly integrate all the extreme and heightened material we are receiving, so our memories, feelings, and the energy of the moment get repressed. Unless we do trauma healing, this material will have to be stored in the body, hidden away, and lived over. Billy's midnight bender is a coping mechanism. It's a way for him to deal with the results of traumatic events that happened long ago, including the physical and sexual assault he experienced when his family was living overseas, the sudden death of his sister when he was a teenager, and his parents' subsequent divorce. He has developed this addiction to protect himself from the unbearable pain he's accumulated throughout his life, and he's not aware of how slippery the slope is. While we can't change what happened, we can change how his brain, body, and soul experience the emotions, feelings, sensations, and soul loss he suffers from in the present day. But first, we have to keep him alive. So I have to go find him. I have to get my exhausted ass up and get in the car and go driving around LA looking for him. To be clear, I do not go out looking for clients on a regular basis. Not that I wouldn't, it's just that it doesn't work so well. Most of the time, *they* need to be the ones to reach out. They have to be *ready* for the help. And usually they need to come down from the drugs to realize they are ready. That they are finally done, that they truly want to make a change.

But in rare circumstances, I get a sixth sense that something bad is going to happen if I don't intervene. Billy has been an addict for nine years. Like most addicts, once the substance is in his body he loses his ability to say no. For Billy, that looks like alcohol segueing into marijuana segueing into heroin or meth—or both. His underlying trauma has at times bubbled over into suicidal ideation, and it could go there again to-night. He needs a loving safety net to catch him. It can't wait until morning.

I stick my head in the door of the guest room and tell Mom I'm leaving to go to work.

"At 11:30 p.m.? But *why*?" she asks.

"I'm going to fight dragons," I reply. It's a phrase my team and I use for the after-dark calls: the direct encounters with addiction, mental illness, and, hardest of all, their cousin psychosis.

I'm barely out the door when I get a call from Billy's dad: Billy may be at a gas station over the hill. As I jump in the car I'm already calling two guys who work for me. I might need backup to get Billy into the car and safely transported to detox. Jack is a sober coach who plays various different roles in helping to support our clients. I also call our security guard Ben, who used to be a Navy SEAL. They're on the way. Now I have to make the harder decision: do I bring in the police now, or do I try first with just myself and my team? It's tricky, because once you call the police, a lot of things are out of your hands. But if you know someone is using hard drugs and driving a car and may be suicidal, you may not have time to spare. Am I willing to risk it? I take a deep breath and a moment to pause for the right decision to come. I call Karen, my second-in-command, and we talk it through. I choose the police. The police get there faster than I do, and they call to say they do not see him or the car. I call Karen back, and she is in direct communication with Jack and Ben and tells them to meet me at a gas station in the Valley. This is where Billy was last seen, so I want to see for myself if he is still there.

I'm updating Billy's parents from the road, but I'm not giving them too much information. The constant ups and downs are too much for any parent. Just the facts, until I have more to say. I'd first heard from his parents four years ago, when they called me after Billy had relapsed and was in detox. They'd heard I could help them find a residential treatment center after he left the detox center. I've been their go-to ever since.

Most families don't know what they don't know about treatment, and the addiction recovery system in the United States is—to put it mildly—a complicated mess. Lacking a calm and knowledgeable captain asking the right questions and running point, families make quick decisions that are often not optimized for long-term recovery. This is where I come in. As a crisis recovery manager, it's my job to know what they couldn't possibly know and give them the guidance they need to take action.

When they hear my job title, clients and their families assume they know what I do—mostly based on past experiences they've had, or what they've seen on TV. But rarely do they understand the breadth of what I offer, so I have a little speech I roll out to explain.

"I'm an attorney," I begin. "I also have my doctorate in depth psychology, with a focus on trauma and neuroscience. I'm certified in alcohol and drug counseling and Soul Psychology. For a dozen years I was an agent and partner at one of the largest Hollywood talent agencies. But then I left to build my company, Recovery Management Agency or RMA, which is a recovery service on the talent agency model. We offer the full range of services and resources our clients need to heal from trauma, end their struggles with addiction and mental illness, and go on to live big, beautiful lives. We combine short- and long-term treatment based on their soul's plan. It's a fusion of modalities I call Soulbriety."

Usually the response to this talk is something along the lines of *I didn't even know anyone did what you do.* We provide not just a plan for recovery but a holistic plan for Soulbriety. A Soulbriety plan always starts with understanding the story of the client's soul. From there we identify trauma points, conduct mental health assessments, and research options for the most appropriate treatment. We then draft a plan for up to a year of recovery. I say "draft" because a Soulbriety plan is always getting updated. As the client recovers and earns a seat at the table, they begin to participate along with the treatment team on what remains to be healed and how to move forward.

It's taken me some time to get all the right resources in place to be able to roll out the first draft of a plan at a moment's notice. We have to work quickly because by the time people find me, they're usually at the end of their rope. This doesn't necessarily mean they've hit "rock bottom"—thankfully. In today's world of designer drugs and prescription pills, "rock bottom" often looks like psychosis, overdose, or death. There's something to be said for getting off the elevator at the fourth floor like a lady or gentleman, and not having to go all the way to the basement. But they've usually been on the elevator for a while, riding up and down, trying to find the right people, the right options, and the right resources for their particular soul's journey. By the time people find me and RMA, they are ready to get off. So we pride ourselves on being ready. We dive right in, doing assessments with pertinent family members and colleagues, and reading about all previous treatment—medical files, discharge paperwork, and more. Then we come back with a treatment plan that includes both short-term and long-term components. In addition, we've got lawyers, on-call security, private travel options, and clinical connections. We stay current on residential treatment centers and therapeutic boarding schools and can get the neuropsychiatric testing necessary for an accurate diagnosis. We've even got clients covered if they have to leave their house for months: we'll negotiate with their landlords, sell their houses if needed, find temporary homes for pets, handle the move, and get all their belongings safely into storage. And once they are out of treatment, we help them get back into school, choose a vocation if needed, and create a sense of autonomy, self-reliance, and financial independence.

We've helped Billy in exactly these ways over the last four years. But today, we're back in crisis management mode. I am gathering and filing away lots of new information, but my only task tonight is to find Billy and get him somewhere medically safe. After he begins to stabilize, we'll start thinking about next steps. Weigh in about what happened, assess his willingness to seek treatment, and help his parents set new boundaries.

I meet up with the guys and we all get into one car. Karen needs my attention. She's been tracking down Billy's friend Jane, who she's finally gotten on the phone. Yes, Billy is supposed to come to her house later. But no, she won't tell Karen where she lives. She's afraid we'll come and get him, which is of course exactly what we are planning to do. I text Billy's mom to call Jane. She does and tells Jane she just wants to know where he will be staying the night. Jane relents, and we have the address.

Soon we're parked outside Jane's house, and we wait. We wait and we wait and we wait. As we do, I consider putting on my invisible, protective cloak. It's a visualization a mentor of mine suggested when I told her how energetically depleted I could get on these calls. She told me to imagine wearing a protective cloak: head-to-toe virtual coverage, including a hood. I was skeptical, but I tried it. And to my surprise, it worked. It somehow allows me to hold in the energy I need, and not have it sucked out by the situation. Wearing the cloak, I feel more in control of my internal light. Over time the visualization has developed its own alter ego: in certain circumstances, I flip the cloak over in my mind's eye and it suddenly becomes a superhero cape. Still protective, but leaving my arms free to extend light and love where needed. Tonight is one of those nights. Billy needs all the support he can get, and so do I. I choose the cape.

Finally, at 2 a.m., I see his car pull up down the street. He parks but doesn't get out. I tell the team I'm going over there. I ask Jack to come too, but to trail behind a bit, which is not the norm. Usually security goes first; you never know what you're going to encounter. Addict, dark street, activated trauma. Best to be safe rather than sorry. But Billy has never been violent, and I know him well. As I walk up to the car, Billy opens the door and gets out. He sees me and becomes a deer in headlights. I can feel that he's shocked to see me, but also that he's flooded by shame. He's high on methamphetamine and heroin. He's holding a needle in his hand. And—this is new—he's dressed top to bottom like a woman.

"I can't believe you're seeing me like this," he says, looking away.

"Why?" I ask, glancing at the needle in his hand. We both know he's a drug addict, after all.

"No, not that," he says, shaking his head. "I mean . . . dressed like this." I see tears welling in his eyes.

"Yeah," I say. "I understand." He hangs his head, the tears spilling over his mascaraed eyelashes.

"Because, Billy," I continue, "that shirt is hideous. Please let me take you shopping."

Billy looks up at me, and while he's too far gone to laugh, he's able to make eye contact again. Some of the shame has lifted off. *The power of humor.*

I make a mental note to revise Billy's Soulbriety Plan to make space for this part of him, a part that clearly wants and needs expression. But that will come later. For now, all I can do is witness. Witness, and get him sober.

It takes thirty minutes of sitting with him in his car to talk him into letting us take him to detox. He tries to vac-illate, but we don't accept it. He's given us the first okay. Once you get that first okay, you hold on to it and keep the train moving. Most addicts will try to get out of their first yes, so you just act like you can't hear them anymore. We operate from the yes we got five seconds or five minutes or five hours ago. That said, Billy does have a request. Actually, two. He wants to change back into jeans and a T-shirt before he walks into detox—fair enough, he has them right there in the car. And also, he wants to shoot up one more time. This one is a tough call. I can't take the needle away from him and he won't get out of his car until he uses. Jack looks at the needle and turns to me. "It's okay," he says. "Go wait in your car."

Once Billy's finished, he and Jack join me in my car and we drive away. "Where are we going?" he asks me. Now his jaw is grinding from left to right and I can feel his pain as the speed runs through his veins sitting in the back seat of this small car we are all jammed into together. It is a small private detox connected to a hospital here in the Valley. We will be there in ten minutes. I actually think it might take us twenty minutes, but I know that feeling of being in the car high and just wanted to get to the destination and get out and do more drugs. I look over at Jack with tears in my eyes. He nods that recognition that all addicts have where we understand the pain of others at a soul level. We have been where Billy is now, maybe in a different set of circumstances with different drugs but the same feelings, the deep shame, self-disgust, an unbearable pull toward the darkest part of yourself, and the unrelenting torture of your soul breaking apart again and again.

CHAPTER TWO

Respecting the Symptoms

Emily is twenty-six years old and has been trying to get sober from drugs and alcohol for a long time. Her psychiatrist connected us, knowing that Emily needs more help than she is currently getting. The first day we meet, we go for Chinese food—her favorite. She's at least twenty pounds underweight, her hair is falling out, and her skin is gray. Not a hint of gray, but truly gray. Ashen. The soul shines its light through the eyes; Emily's internal light is close to extinction. Her eyes are vacant, clouded, but I never turn away. I want to see if she can connect. If there is a small flicker of hope or fight in her.

While I wait for eye contact, I tell her the truth. I let her know I see how bad things are. That she needs help immediately, that she is very sick. I am afraid that if she doesn't do something to get into recovery from her addiction—let alone all the underlying trauma—she will die. I ask her if she wants to die. This is the first time she looks right at me. Answering with conviction, she says: *No*. I ask her if she needs help. *Yes*.

Here is a woman who has been trying to get sober for years. But in all that time, in all those therapy and psychiatry offices, had anyone ever asked her the story of her life? The story of her soul? *Tell me your story*, I say. *Start from the beginning.*

Two hours later, I am sitting with a catalogue of suffering. Emily has endured what I consider a string of "dark nights," each of which is powerful enough to fuel considerable soul loss. Starting at a very young age, she was more sensitive than the average child. Before the age of six, she lived with an addict mother—who would often hit or slap her when she had been drinking too much—and a father who suffered from bipolar disorder and had frequent manic episodes where he would rage and be verbally abusive. Emily had been taken out of her home five times and put into temporary foster care because of abuse and neglect. Without parents who provided consistent and reliable comfort and safety, Emily developed an attachment disorder—in her case, insecure attachment. This disorder affects her ability to regulate her mood, to maintain nourishing relationships, and to feel a sense of belonging. It also makes her statistically predisposed to self-harm, addiction, and suicidal ideology. With all of these factors, Emily started early to believe she was less than, not lovable, and—with all the ailments she was dealing with—broken. She's not broken, she's just brimming with trauma and toxic stress. The origin of which comes, in large part, from her very high ACEs score.

The Adverse Childhood Experiences Study as conducted by the CDC and Kaiser Permanente in the 1990s assessed how the ten most common childhood "stressors"—physical abuse, sexual abuse, emotional abuse, physical neglect, emotional neglect, mental illness, parental incarceration, divorce or other loss of a parent, substance abuse, and domestic violence—impacted a person's health and well-being later in life. (Other adverse experiences of consequence include poverty, discrimination, lack of housing availability, and community violence.) The study revealed that the higher the number of adverse childhood experiences (ACEs) reported, the higher was the individual's risk of developing physical and mental illness or addiction, as well as being at greater risk of further traumatic experiences and suicide. In 2019, data from the CDC revealed that 61 percent of adults have experienced at least one ACE—placing them at an "intermediate risk" of developing physical and mental illnesses including heart disease, cancer, respiratory diseases, depression, and diabetes later in life. One in six adults has experienced four or more ACEs, which places them at a "very high risk" of these issues. Moreover, the study showed that racial and ethnic minorities and those with lower socioeconomic status were at an even greater risk for experiencing a high number of ACEs—and increased health risks as a result. (To take the quiz yourself, please see the Resources section at the end of this book.) Of course, many people who have experienced these stressors never see health consequences and in fact are able to thrive. Even siblings who grew up in the same household may have very different outcomes depending on their age, gender, birth order, psychological resilience, and genetics. But the risks to those with high ACE scores remain, and research continues to determine why some children are more likely to be affected than others.

The legacy of ACEs is toxic stress, a prolonged chronic stress that can harm both the brain and the body. Not even loving, protective families can shield children from all of these ACEs, such as the death of a parent, illness, or a divorce. They may not have the resources or support to handle their own mental health or addiction issues, in spite of the trauma these destabilizing forces can generate for the children they love. Or in the case of racial discrimination or lack of sufficient housing, the parents may not be able to protect their children since the trauma is theirs as well.

When I ask a client to tell me their story, what I am listening for is not a direct narrative of a traumatic event. Most of the time the client is either unaware of their trauma or is unable to remember the details. Instead, I am looking for them to tell me the story of their life, seen through their eyes. I don't even mention the word "trauma." It's usually too soon in our process for that word. But I can see trauma's footprint, even if we're not talking about it directly. I've been trained to look for the physiological signs of dissociation, overwhelm, and memory loss. I carefully feel for subtle emotional responses that the client may not even know they're feeling. Any whiff of unspoken grief, rage, hopelessness, or shame, and I know something happened in the past that has not yet been healed. I also look for symptoms of addiction, depression, anxiety, or physical conditions—the latter most often related to the "center of the person": her gut, heart, and lungs.

As a soul-centered practitioner, what I'm looking for under all of these outward signs is soul loss. Understanding where my client is disconnected from her own essence is essential as I put together her Soulbriety plan. The story is only a means of finding the ruptures that will later require tending and healing. But for now, with Emily, my role is simply to witness the disconnect from soul. Listening to her narrative helps me build rapport; by listening to her memories, I can help hold what she's been carrying. To make sure telling the story is not retraumatizing, I ask her to stick to highlights rather than the details. I tell her to imagine herself reading a newspaper, only giving me the headlines, and maybe the bylines. Never the full article.

Today, Emily lives with her adoptive parents, Mike and Tina, who have been caring for her since she was seven years old. I call them after lunch and let them know how severe her addiction has become. They say it's fine for her to take the rest of the summer to work on her mental health, but that she needs to be ready to go back to college in the fall. She is only a semester away from graduating, they tell me, and she needs to take her MCATs no later than October. I silently shake my head, but I'm not surprised. It's hard for families and loved ones to see the situation as clearly as I do. Addiction and mental health issues creep in slowly, until one day you do not recognize the person in front of you. Loved ones scan everything the patient says or does for evidence that there's hope—any hint that they are trying to overcome the addiction, or that they are having a good day or even just a good hour. They then lock their hearts onto that moment, holding on to it for dear life, using it as evidence that everything is going to be fine. I understand of course; imagining the worst about someone you love is too heartbreaking. So even while families are afraid their loved one is going to die, they often also have a false sense of security. They think that as long as they're watching carefully, checking in regularly, their child will not be in danger.

So I'm not surprised when her parents say, *Thank you for your help, we're going to wait and see how things go, she needs to finish classes, and she just started seeing her therapist again.* But I also know it isn't going to be enough.

Emily's parents believe with all their hearts that continued academic success is essential for her to make her way in life. They were not fortunate enough to have access to a higher level of education when they were growing up, and they believe it's a make-or-break requirement for Emily's future. I see this all the time: parents who mistake education as a safety net that cannot be forgone. While it is true that college education provides enormous benefits on some career paths, I've seen the pressure to complete college—especially in students who don't genuinely enjoy school and whose joy is unlikely to be found in a future office job—cause more harm than good. For some young people, mental health and recovery *must* come before education, or the education itself will be wasted.

The desire parents have to save their child via external means—focusing on getting good grades, degrees, and the perfect job, rather than encouraging them to do their inner work—is an inadvertent reach for the easier, softer way. It's the parental equivalent to Emily reaching for the drugs: an external fix for internal pain. When the soul is aching, nothing on the outside will help. Emily has to grow down, illuminate her soul, find her authentic self, and co-create a life in step with her soul. A life that allows her to be who she is *meant* to be, which may or may not be the doctor her parents *want* her to be.

Emily's parents are aware of Emily's early childhood trauma, including the trauma of adoption itself. They told her she was adopted when she was old enough to understand, and according to them, it has never been a problem for her. But when something happens to a child before they have the language to express how they feel—also known as preverbal trauma—they may never develop the words to explain what's going on inside. Raised by Mike and Tina, Emily is impacted by their beliefs, emotions, and childhood wounds in addition to those of her birth parents. While Mike and Tina certainly want the best for her, they are running that desire through their own filters—which may not be right for Emily.

So when I work with a young adult who is still dependent on their parents, I do full assessments on each member of the system to understand how unhealed trauma may be impacting the family soul. In this case, Emily's dad comes from a military family and was in the military himself. Feelings were often swept aside in his childhood home; the family motto was "pull yourself up by your bootstraps and get to work." Emily's mom's family of origin was filled with dysfunction and chaos due to alcoholic parents. When she met Emily's father, she was attracted to his buttoned-up style. They married at a young age, and she felt sure with the security he provided she would be able to give her daughter a different life. Knowing this information, I better understand how they parent and why.

When a crisis affects a family, it's easy for the system to point the finger at the identified patient. But the culprit here is not Emily; the family system as a whole is suffering from trauma lying beneath the surface. I will take this into account as I get Emily the care she needs, guiding her parents to do their own work alongside hers. Only when the entire family agrees to do their trauma work can the system be healed.

Emily's parents, for now, decide to take the easy route. They focus on getting Emily back to school, kicking the can a little farther down the road.

It only takes a few weeks before they call. They are really worried now, and they want us to go by Emily's college apartment and check on her. They are worried she's using drugs again, as they just got a call from her friend saying she missed the MCAT exam that morning. I send one of my associates, Anna, over to the house to check in. When Anna calls she tells me Emily is definitely high on cocaine and other stimulant medication. Not only that, she appears to be psychotic and paranoid, which can happen from repeated cocaine use for a few days in a row. She's holding a knife and threatening to leave the apartment and go kill her mother.

Anna is able to get Emily to put the knife down, and she takes away Emily's car keys. Satisfied that she's not going to *actually* kill her mom, I see the upside to this turn of events: we finally have an opportunity to get her help.

Thirty years ago when I put my mom in the hospital, all I had to do was trick her into thinking I was driving her to a boat where Victor Kiriakis was waiting. Today it's anything but easy to get a psychotic person forcibly checked into a hospital. In order to place someone on a psychiatric hold against their will in California they need to be threatening to hurt themselves or someone else, and they need to have a plan. Emily had said the magic words: "I want to kill someone" (in this case, her mom) "and I have a plan for how I'm going to do it" (in this case, with a knife). While I'd prefer to call the Department of Health and have clinicians come by, I know that not all mental health units can write involuntary holds—which we're going to need. The police can. So I call 911 and head over in my car to wait. I am outside Emily's apartment when the police *and* paramedics, including an ambulance, show up.

My phone rings. *Shit.* It's my niece FaceTiming me. I try to never press "decline" for either her or her brother. I try to always show up, as a living amends to my family. So I answer, but I position the phone away from the emergency vehicles that begin to arrive. I am pleased to see that 911 decided to send both the police and ambulance. When calling 911 it is important to be very detailed as to what is going on in order to hopefully ensure the proper response team. Otherwise, we would be waiting in her apartment with the police while they reached out to an ambulance or mental health team if deemed necessary. I greet her and tell her how happy I am to see her. But I also tell her I am dealing with a work emergency. She may only be fifteen, but she gets it. So she smiles and wishes me luck, and after asking me to be careful, she hangs up.

I flip my invisible cloak into a cape and head into the building with the rest of them. As I squeeze into the tiny elevator with a dozen of the first responders, I quickly tell them Emily's story. I have to go about it carefully, since I know there are differences between the way preexisting mental illness and substance-induced psychosis get treated. Preexisting mental illness might include bipolar or major depression, an anxiety disorder such as obsessive compulsive disorder, a thought disorder such as schizophrenia, a personality disorder such as borderline or antisocial, or some combination.

It's treated as a health issue, a medical issue. It's often consid-ered something that the patient can't control.

Substance-induced psychosis, conversely, is looked at dif-ferently. While it's well-known that addiction is a disease, many people still look upon it as something the patient had control over. That the psychosis is somehow their fault, and they should have known better than to continue using.

So I overshare about Emily's background in an effort to get them to treat her with the same level of dignity and re-spect as any medical patient they might encounter. I request that the officers come into the apartment one at a time, given she has extreme trauma. I tell them she has a painful back in-jury and they need to be very careful if they have to restrain her. They are uninterested in what I have to say and proceed to enter the apartment as an entourage. Emily faints at the sight of them. I run toward her but the EMTs push me out of the way. They pick her up and forcibly try to seat her in an emergency chair so they can wheel her down to the street. She wakes and begins to kick and punch and scream like a wild animal. She is terrified. To her, the psychosis is real, and the police are scary. I try to intervene and be a calming voice but they pull me aside. Soon I am begging them to be careful, not to hurt her. They are doing the best they can, but this is a lot of burly men in uniforms around a ninety-pound girl. I am reminded that trauma-informed care is still limited in the emergency field. Finally they get her strapped in and we head down to the ambulance, with Emily screaming the whole way. Once she is in the ambulance they give her a sedative, and I ask the driver to take her to the UCLA hospital. They remind me they are not an Uber—they take patients to the designated hospital for the jurisdiction where the call was made. I plead with them: her psychiatrist is at UCLA, and they have the best psychiatric department. Since the state of California closed all the mental hospitals decades ago, there are very few hospitals to choose from and fewer still that have the kind of care I want for Emily. In the end they agree, and I sit in the front of the ambulance, texting.

First, I contact Emily's psychiatrist to keep her in the loop. Then I call the hospital, preparing security to come and meet us at the ambulance bay. I arrange for her to have a private psychiatric room in the ER while we await her clearance for a 5150, which is code in California for a temporary involuntary psychiatric commitment to the hospital. This could take hours; most of the time it takes all day. I stay there the whole time, talking to doctors, to Emily's parents, to the ER staff. Making sure everything gets handled. Never leaving her to feel alone. Management of traumatic situations like this one requires exquisite care, something most people simply do not get. But I know how important it is because it was something I myself did *not* receive when I needed it many years earlier.

—

"CAN I HAVE some candy?" I would ask Duppy, my grandmother on my mom's side. Duppy is like a second mother to me. She has a warm, cuddling way about her. While I'm growing up, she and her husband, my Poppy, live only a few minutes from my house. Which works for my mom, who depends heavily on Duppy and speaks to her multiple times a day—filling her in on the events of our lives, especially as they relate to my sister and me. Duppy is Mom's biggest confidante, and mom asks her advice on pretty much everything—vacillating between being a kid whose parents live down the street and being a parent herself. Duppy is much more of a co-parent for me and my sister than my dad is. Mom seems unsure of herself, as if she's making things up along the way, and Duppy's support is her lifeline.

Duppy works downstairs in the apartment building they live in, as the building manager, and we're over there all the time. Going to her office is always a big treat. I love running in and jumping into her lap, snuggling up against her great big boobs. She gives the best hugs I've ever had.

"Of course, darling," she says, about the candy. "The sweets are for you." I stick my little hand into the candy jar that sits on her desk and take out a handful. Butterscotch suckers and Tootsie Rolls are my favorite, but I like it all. Sugar is always there, from the very beginning. Our house is filled with it: chocolate, cake, ice cream. More sugar than actual food. (If a kid today were to have as much access to all those sweets, it would probably be considered neglect.) Living off chocolate and soda is my first addiction.

But then comes alcohol, the summer I am sixteen. Until now I've never really had alcohol, but this year my best friend, Wendy, and I go to a summer program at Tufts University. It's like summer camp meets college, but with less oversight. One afternoon Wendy and I are sitting on the grass sunning ourselves, the way you used to in the '80s. You know, covered in baby oil and lying in direct UV sunlight. That's when I see him.

"Wendy!" I say. "There he is, over there!" I'm pointing at a boy named Scott. To me he looks as handsome as Jake Ryan in *Sixteen Candles*, leaning against his red Porsche waiting for

Samantha to come out of the church after her sister's wedding. (I was always into movies, even back then.) Scott is talking to a beautiful blond girl with gigantic boobs. I look down at my own skinny body and sigh. I have no idea how I could compete, how I would even try.

The following weekend everyone is going to an outdoor concert. I have some friends visiting me from high school, and they've brought alcohol with them. Someone mixes vodka and juice, and the next thing I know, it's the middle of the night and I'm lying on the ground in wet grass. In my half-unconscious state I realize someone is standing over me. Squinting, I see it's none other than Jake Ryan.

"Oh, hi, Scott," I say, aiming for my best sexy-flirty voice but landing somewhere closer to drunken slurring.

"Are you okay?" he asks. "Let me take you up to your room. Where are your keys?"

"Keys?" I ask him back, as if he just asked me the meaning of life. *Is Scott actually going to take me back to my room?*

A few minutes of him feeling around in the grass in the complete dark—this is way before iPhones, with their convenient flashlights—he yells, "Got 'em!" He helps me up and I can barely contain my excitement. I'm suddenly more sober, able to envision the love story that is, I'm sure, about to unfold. He helps me all the way upstairs, unlocks the dorm room door, and guides me inside. As we approach the bed, I feel so excited I think I'm going to burst.

And burst I do . . . vomiting right down the front of Scott's jeans. He doesn't say much, just helps me clean up, leaves the trash can next to the bed, waves goodnight, and closes the door behind him.

"Wendy!" I exclaim when I wake up the next morning. "Scott and I had the *best* night together! He was like Prince Charming, rescuing and taking care of me!"

And so it is, for the version of me who's been looking to fill the gaping hole in her heart for a very long time. For before addiction is a problem, it often looks like a solution. And that summer I discover that alcohol, plus a man to save me, is a reasonable approximation of love.

I return to Great Neck for my senior year of high school, to find my Duppy living with us. I know she is dying, but it's not a topic we discuss as a family. She's in a hospital bed in the living room, hooked up to a bunch of machines to keep her comfortable. My parents tell us to act normal; they explain that she's there because she enjoys being in the house and being a part of our everyday lives. Detaching from the severity of Duppy's condition, I don't notice the steady decline in my mother at the same time.

I fall in love that year—probably the most honest, pure love I've ever had, even to this day—with a boy named Todd. He adores me and wants to spend all his free time with me. He and his family make me feel taken care of, which is something I haven't felt in years. It's well timed, since my Duppy dies that year. It is a loss my mother is not equipped to handle on her own, and it sends her into a downward spiral. While I am medicating with alcohol and Todd, she has turned to the medicine cabinet. Looking back, it's easy to see why. She's burdened by the pain of a marriage that is over and is secretly in love with another man. She is grieving the loss of her mother, who has been her primary support system forever. Heartbreak, grief, and yearning for love are all that she can feel. Like most of us, she's never been taught that this kind of emotional rupture is an opportunity to look more deeply at herself, to grow down into herself and encounter her soul. Instead, she copes as she knows how: she picks up the phone and requests prescriptions for anti-anxiety medications, which the doctor down the block is happy to provide.

At the end of senior year, Wendy and I get into the University of Michigan. We are of course going to be roommates. Todd, however, is going to Wisconsin. On my eighteenth birthday I hug him goodbye at JFK Airport. I hold onto him as tightly as I can, as the tears roll down my face. I can feel his body tremble against mine. Will anyone ever love me this much again? Will I ever feel this safe again? I know deep in my bones that something will change the minute he gets on the plane.

"I love you," he says.

"I love you, too," I choke out between sobs.

"I will see you soon, and I will visit," he promises. "I love you more than anything and anyone, and I always will." And with that, he is gone, and I am left alone in the airport.

In spite of the pain—or maybe because of it—I am ready to go to college. Ready to leave the turmoil, chaos, and sadness of Duppy's death behind. Of course, I now see that all that pain, all that trauma, all those feelings are packed right up in my duffel bags with the rest of my things. But unaware of the soul loss at my core, I think I am ready to live, laugh, and celebrate my newfound freedom. Looking back, I see both peaks and valleys—the ways in which college *does* feed my soul, and the ways in which it becomes the perfect place for me to hone the skill of suppressing loss, loneliness, and fear with heavy alcohol use. I drink to fit in. I drink to feel connected. I drink to feel whole, and at the same time calm. But most truthfully, I drink to get drunk. That is the sole purpose of alcohol for me. I don't like the taste, but I like how "me" I feel when I drink.

Without Todd, I've lost another of my coping mechanisms: love, belonging, and comfort. So it's no surprise that I find his replacement approximately twelve hours after I arrive at Michigan.

When we find our dorm room, the sign on the door says *Alyssa Hallerman*—another offense in a lifetime of egregious misspellings of my name. I decide at that moment that this will be the last one. Elisa no more, I christen myself *Lisa Hallerman* from that moment on. A new name for a new era in my life.

Wendy and I are still unpacking our matching lavender bed sets when I have to pee. I go searching for the one all-girls bathroom on our floor, and on the way back, I see him.

I run all the way back to our room and burst through the door.

"Wendy! *Wendy!* OMG! It's Scott!"

"Scott who?" she says.

"Scott-Scott! Tufts Scott! He's here! He's down the hall!"

"*No way!*" she says, as surprised as I am. Like the mischievous besties we are, we concoct the perfect excuse to go talk to him. We're casually looking for a hammer to hang something on the wall, we decide. We head down to the boys' side of the sixth floor of the Mary Markley dorm and knock on his door. There he is, still Jake Ryan but now with a little more of a bad boy vibe, looking like Springsteen in his jeans and white T-shirt. This is fate. This is destiny. He will be mine.

The red flags pile up from day one. While there is genuine friendship, attraction, and love, there is also alcohol—lots and lots of it. And for Scott, drugs as well. He's a fighter when he is high, so we're always getting kicked out of bars and concerts, and I spend a lot of hours in the waiting room at the local hospital. His rage stems from his own childhood ruptures, and it's a perfect match for my need for familiar feelings of disorganized, unpredictable attachment.

By the end of sophomore year, it's too much. I tell Scott we're on a break, and my other college roommate Steph and I spend the summer taking classes at UCLA. As soon as we move into the dorms, we meet the guys who live next door. Marc—tall and handsome, with a smile that could light up the room—catches my eye. We start seeing each other, and over the course of the summer I really start to fall for him. We continue dating long distance when I'm back at Michigan that fall, and our relationship feels easy—he's trustworthy, I feel safe, and we genuinely love each other. It's an unfamiliar feeling for me, and I start to miss the chaos and drama. When Scott shows up on my doorstep again, I break up with Marc and head back into the comfortably tumultuous relationship. Bonded by our childhood wounds, and yet to do any internal repair, Scott and I get caught in a never-ending cycle of love and turmoil that will continue for eight more years.

—

DURING THIS TIME, the steadiest relationship I have is alcohol. It offers me a sense of freedom. I am free to be myself, uninhibited. I feel beautiful, charming, and brilliant. I manage to shed my flaws at the bottom of a drink. All I need to make my insecurities disappear is to refill the glass. But that liberty is fleeting; you can only escape from soul loss for so long before you start to abandon your dreams.

After graduation, I want nothing more than to move to Los Angeles. My nostalgia for that summer at UCLA is real; I associate LA with joy, freedom, and love. (Not to mention sunshine and the beach.) My soul is sending a strong signal, but my head isn't listening. Instead, I move back to New York City, get a tiny studio, and get ready for law school—because that's what Scott is doing. Scott, who gives me the illusion of safety and security, which to me is a rough equivalent for love. I don't even want to be a lawyer, but I am happy to be relieved of the burden of figuring out what I *do* want. I'll just do what the boy in my life is doing, and that will be that.

My first year I'm going through the motions of school; I can already tell I am not interested in law. My soul pleads with me to change course, but I continue to drown out its wisdom with alcohol. The summer after my first year I spend my days at the beach, going out every night. My friends are starting to get engaged and starting to settle down while I care only about having a great time and keeping everyone entertained with my crazy antics. Then toward the end of the summer, I get a call from my sister.

"Something is wrong with Mom, you need to come home," she says. Home means Great Neck, New York, which is about thirty minutes away from the city, out on Long Island. It's where my parents still live, still married. "The house has been chaotic and Mom is a mess. Everything has escalated and Dad is unwilling to face the severity of the situation."

"What do you mean, is she sick?" I ask.

"It's bad," she says. "Just please come home now!"

As I sit on the train, I remember the conversation I'd had with Mom a month earlier, over the Fourth of July weekend. "Mom, I know something is going on with you and another man," I had said, repeating what my sister had told me. Unlike me, she has had a front-row seat to the last four years of Mom's addiction and affair. "We are not mad. We understand you aren't happy with Dad anymore. But please tell him. All the lying and sneaking around is driving us crazy."

"*You're* crazy!" Mom had insisted. "Nothing is going on! There is nothing to talk about."

But as my sister and I climb the red spiral staircase to the second floor of my childhood home, there is no more denying the issue. We enter her bedroom—her sanctuary, her dark cave—to find a frail woman, weighing maybe eighty pounds, sitting up in bed.

"Mom, what's going on?" I say.

"Hi!" she says.

"Mom, what is going on? What's wrong?" I demand.

"Hi, there!" she says again, as if seeing me for the first time. She proceeds to talk to us about a trip she's planning, a trip on a boat. She is going with Victor Kiriakis, Marlena, and of course Bo and Hope—the characters from the soap opera *Days of Our Lives*. I cannot really comprehend what is happening or why.

"Mom, do you know who I am?"

"Nope," she replies cheerfully. "But hi! How are you?" Very polite she is, but clearly not in our universe.

"Mom, do you know who *you* are?" I ask delicately.

"Yes!" she replies with confidence. "I'm Batman!"

SOULBRIETY

We go straight to my dad, who is downstairs watching TV on the brown leather couch.

"Dad, we have to take Mom to the hospital," I announce.

"No," he says. I glance at my sister and her look says it all. *This is what I've been dealing with while you've been away.* My heart breaks for her, for my mom, for my dad—for all of us. To me it feels like Mom's decline has come on so fast. In reality, it's been a slow burn—escalating over the past four years since the death of her mother and her introduction to benzos and barbiturates.

"*Yes*, Dad. Something is wrong," I insist. "We are taking Mom to the hospital. And you can come if you want or not."

With the help of a little white lie—"We have to drive you to the boat!"—we get Mom into the car and drive her to the hospital. Once we have her settled in her room, the doctor pulls us out into the hallway.

"I need to know if she is talking about anything real," he says. "She is insisting on meeting someone named Dan, on a boat. Is Dan a real person?"

Here we go. I look at my dad as he takes a breath and clears his throat.

"I don't know, doctor," he says. "You will have to speak to my daughters." And with that, he excuses himself, leaving his eighteen- and twenty-two-year-old daughters to explain to the doctor that we believe our mom has a boyfriend named Dan.

Just then the phone in the room rings. What do you know, it's Dan.

I leave and go to find my dad.

"We think Mom is having an affair with some man named Dan," I say. Not only does he not seem surprised, he seems numb.

50

"Don't be mad at your mom," he says. "I haven't been the best husband either." What the hell does *that* mean?

"But I'm not staying," he finishes. And with that, he leaves the hospital and never comes back. It's the last meaningful conversation I'll have with him for a long time to come. *Where are the grown-ups?* I think. *Why are there no grown-ups here?*

Each time we experience trauma, whether big or small, it's as if a tiny Post-it Note gets left on our soul. *I should be ashamed of myself. People are untrustworthy. I don't deserve love. As hard as I try, I'll never be enough.* Those Post-its turn into our understanding of who we are; they become part of our narrative, even though they are only a partial, misguided, and—at the very least—*incomplete* version of who we are. In believing these things, we cut ourselves off from parts of ourselves. We lose access to our deepest truths. Our intuition is hijacked. Our authenticity gets buried. And our gifts become clouded by self-doubt, fear, and unworthiness.

When I ask a client if they have experienced trauma they usually say, "No . . . I mean, not *really.*" Then they tell me their story. *My parents got divorced when I was in third grade. We moved cities when I was in high school and I never made friends. My grandpa was taking care of me one day after school, and he had a heart attack and died on the playground in front of me. My best friend moved away when I was in seventh grade. While I was at sleepaway camp, our house burned to the ground. When I was in my late twenties I found out that I had another sibling that my dad never told our family about. My coach told me I needed to lose weight in order to keep up with the other kids. I had a bump on my nose and the boys called me Toucan Sam. My parents fought all the time at night and I still have trouble sleeping. I was on varsity football and just when they were about to make me captain I hurt my knee and had to sit out my senior year. It's foggy but something happened when I was three or four, and I've never really felt comfortable giving anyone hugs since then. A kid in my class died of cancer when I was in fourth grade.*

So why do my clients say "not really" when I ask if they've experienced trauma? Because too often we glance over the hardships we've experienced, dismissing them as "nothing." We think of trauma as being caused by war, disaster, and violence. Which is true, but trauma can also be subtle and chronic. Negative experiences of all shapes and sizes lead to shame, emotional shutdown, low self-esteem, or unexplained physical or mental symptoms. Trauma is a disease of the nervous system, and its genesis is wired deeply in the brain as part of our fight-or-flight response. "Fight or flight" happens when the survival mechanism of the brain kicks in and releases hormones such as cortisol and adrenaline in an effort to protect us. This will inhibit brain function, and your memories of the experience will not be properly integrated. This leaves the traumatized brain unable to connect to your feelings and can make you unable to concentrate or problem solve, stay in the present, and easily set goals and intentions. You are no longer able to adapt and react readily to stimuli in your environment. Your sense of self has been shattered into fragments, leaving you feeling dissociated, anxious, detached, and camouflaged from reality.

GROWING UP ON Long Island, I'm a happy-go-lucky kid. My sister, three-and-a-half years younger than me, is my best friend. We play together all the time, creating an imaginative world of our very own. We make up dance routines and perform them for our parents in the living room. I love to ride my bike around the neighborhood and often play outside after school with my friends. Ice skating is the big after-school activity in my town, so I take lessons and spend Friday nights at the rink skating to music with friends. I'm active and always have a smile on my face. I go to sleepaway camp when I'm nine and it's my happy place. As a family we go on vacations with other families, and there always seems to be a lot of love and joy. But as I head into adolescence, there are subtle changes afoot. Specifically, my parents seem more and more distant. They don't argue or yell—they just don't speak to each other very much anymore. I'm not sure what to make of it.

When I turn thirteen, I am diagnosed with scoliosis. There is a S curvature in my spine that needs to be corrected while I finish growing, so it doesn't get worse. I have to wear a back brace for the next three years, so my mom makes an appointment at the Hospital for Special Surgery to get me fitted. On the day of the appointment, I'm brought into a huge room where a lot of children are being fitted for prosthetics. I am told to stand while a man wraps my body—from my neck down to my pubic bone—with wet plaster strips, over and over again. As the strips begin to dry it feels tight and uncomfortable, and I start to get scared. My mom is crying uncontrollably so I know whatever is happening to me must be horrible. I look to my left and see a boy around eight years old getting his leg wrapped. I look down and see that his leg ends at his knee. I had never seen someone missing a limb before, so I ask the man wrapping me why the boy needs a cast.

"He is getting a prosthetic leg and foot," he tells me, pointing out some prostheses in the corner of the room. Each leg has a different type of shoe or sneaker on it.

"Does his leg hurt?" I ask.

"No, not anymore," he says. His eyes are kind. "He is brave like you."

"He is braver," I say. I still have my feet.

When the cast is removed, Mom and I leave. As soon as we get in the car, she calls Duppy and tells her how horrible the day has been. She's still crying.

"The brace will be so big," she sobs to her mother. "She will have to wear it all the time and everyone will see. What will people *say*? What will the other kids *think*?"

None of these thoughts had even occurred to me, and my mind is spinning. My friends? Why would they care? Why is this such a big deal? The way she's talking makes scoliosis sound horrible—what am I missing? Could it get worse? Will I need prosthetics like that little boy? As I listen to her talk and cry, I'm simultaneously confused and really worried about her. I want to ask her questions, to understand what she is talking about, but I don't want to upset her more. I want to get the hell out of the car but there's nowhere to go. Without options to care for myself, my little body is filling fast with anxiety. Soon I am overwhelmed and unable to speak. What I really need in this moment is a parent, a resourced adult who knows to ask me about my feelings, comfort me, and answer my many questions so I can integrate this difficult experience. Instead—as always—I'm left to worry about someone else's emotions and shut down my own.

On April Fool's Day of that same year, I go to the bathroom and notice a dark stain on my underwear. Terrified—and thinking maybe I am dying—I run down to my mom in the kitchen. When I tell her what I found, she promptly slaps me on my cheek and yells *Congratulations, you're a woman!* Startled and confused, I start to cry. She laughs and explains that I got my period—and just as her mother gave her a congratulatory slap the day she became a woman, so I will one day do the same with my own daughter. I walked away, pushing down my pain, shock, and confusion for lack of a better option.

Moments like this are a part of life. Shocking, but nothing out of the ordinary. There is no obvious trauma: no abuse, no violence, no racial discrimination, no death. But subtly, stressors pile up and begin to create a narrative for a kid. *The world is not safe. No one is going to help you. You need to be vigilant. You are unimaginably vulnerable, so you need to stay small, stay inside the lines, and don't take too many risks.* Even after an obvious trauma, we assume kids will "bounce back" or that they are "too young to remember." And maybe it's true for those who have a very high level of resilience. Resilience is created when the child's caregivers have been attached and attuned. But if the child endured tough situations without explanation, guidance, or management, the feelings don't just go away.

Later, when I'm barely twenty-one years old and Mom is in the psych ward, this pattern rises up again like a tsunami. I'm there visiting her during her two-week stay, before she is coherent enough to be discharged and go directly from the hospital to live with Dan. She somehow gets the idea that a bomb is about to go off "on the boat" (remember, she's living in her own personal version of *Days of Our Lives*) and she needs to flee immediately. As she runs down the hallway, barefoot in her hospital gown, I am able to catch up to her and confront her. I cry and plead with her to return with me to her room, letting her know she is safe in the hospital, safe with me there. She looks right at me but clearly does not recognize me. Terrified, she slaps me hard across the face. Even though I know she's in psychosis, my body seizes up as if she knows exactly what she is doing. In that slap I hear her say: *I don't see you. I can't be there for you. You don't matter and I don't care what you have to say.*

Like all of us, my brain was shaped in early childhood by social and emotional experiences—mostly in response to my parents' actions around me. If our parents or caregivers are not able to manage their own negative and positive states and help us manage ours, our nervous systems will be impacted from then on. Generally speaking, we will have a smaller window of tolerance for emotional intensity, triggering a quicker trauma reaction when a similar situation arises. When the trauma response gets triggered, the body reacts—commonly with feelings of panic, anxiety, and fear. We go into survival mode, which for the nervous system is either fight, flight, or freeze. Since little kids can often neither fight nor flee effectively, they usually end up with a freeze response. While this shutdown feels protective to the psyche, it does not allow the body to release all the survival energy that has risen up.

That unresolved energy gets stored in the body, too often reemerging later in life as physical and mental issues. We go to the doctor complaining of the symptoms: *I have unexplained panic attacks. My back always hurts, in different places every time. I can't get pregnant, even though we've done all the tests and everything is normal. If you could just tell me what's wrong with me.* . . . And the doctors, bless them, do what they're trained to do. Modern medicine focuses on treating symptoms, not their underlying causes. So they prescribe painkillers and exploratory surgery and anti-anxiety medication. (While integrative medicine does seek to understand the root cause of disease, it too often overlooks unhealed past trauma.) While the impacts of trauma on the body are grave and worthy of attention, there is an even deeper story needing to be told. You won't hear about it from medical doctors, for most of them don't even know. And in this case, what they don't know *can* kill you, often long before your physical body meets its final downward slide. Adverse childhood experiences—and traumatic experiences in general—impact more than just the body. They poison our soul.

When we are traumatized, however big or small the incident may seem to us, our soul fragments. To the outer world this appears as psychological dissociation: disconnecting from feelings, thoughts, and memories. This dissociation is a natural and intelligent way to cope with overwhelming intensity when there are no other options. But in the inner realm, the problem goes deeper. When we dissociate from the traumatic event, *we cut off our own awareness of its legacy.* So like a wound that has not been cleaned, medicated, and dressed for healing, it continues to ache outside our awareness. This gaping wound leaves its mark—cutting us off from parts of ourselves, freezing our operating system at the moment of the traumatic incident, and consigning the emotions and sensations we could not feel at the time to linger in our nervous system like a shadow. Yet where do we turn to heal these soul-level wounds? There is no doctor specializing in soul illness. No one yet offers a prescription to heal the soul, feed it, and re-awaken your inner knowing.

There is another loss that compounds the effect of this fragmentation. For it is the soul that makes meaning out of our personal narrative. When we dissociate from our stories of trauma, we unknowingly dissociate from this meaning-making as well. To thrive at the levels of mind, body, and soul, we must remember, integrate, understand, and tell our stories. When the past holds our nervous systems hostage, it effec-tively means our *souls* are broken. A soul that's been shattered does not want simply to be fixed; it wants to be acknowledged. It wants us to see, feel, and never forget that *something import-ant has happened and we will never be the same again.* The soul wants us to willingly observe its fragmentation to appreciate the beauty inside of the pain. By witnessing ourselves at this depth we curate an unshakable sense of who we are and a closer connection to soul than we ever had before.

But to bear witness, we have to make a conscious decision to override our freeze response, to return to the traumatic moments and process what did not get felt back then. Un-less we do, these wounds—seemingly dormant beneath their frozen scabs—will never stop festering. In everyday life, they get picked and poked unknowingly by our day-to-day interac-tions. Often we feel burned by those around us, who have un-knowingly bumped up against our deepest pain. Without the proper medicine, these lacerations become bigger and deeper, and we have no choice but to numb ourselves with our addic-tion. What we don't know—what no one tells us—is that we are suffering a disease of the lost self.

In order to live a soulful life, the life we are meant for, we have to be in sync with our inner wisdom. This inner knowing is the access to our true self. When we listen to it, foster it, follow its lead, we expand more and more into our core-most identity. When we are soul sick, however, we close off from this wellspring of inspiration—losing access to our intuition, passions, and desires. That inner voice is our most trustworthy ally, providing the only authentic guidance we have toward our unique life expression. There is another pathway, thankfully: we can choose willingly to feel. We can decide that no matter how painful, we will let all of our experiences—good and bad, pleasurable and painful—penetrate and deeply affect us. This means summoning the courage to face our past, our trauma, our soul wounds with open eyes and a brave heart. To walk through the pain to the other side and collect the gifts of growing down. Operating in unison with soul allows us to live deeply and be fully present with our intuition, inner wisdom, and sense of home and safety. In harmony with soul, we are in possession of our true power.

 ⸚

IT FEELS LIKE I've lost both my parents in different ways that weekend. Everything I'd believed to be true has been turned on its head. Suddenly all my trust in connection is lost. Connection to my parents, to myself, and to the rest of the relationships in my life. Over the following weeks and months I'll adopt many toxic patterns to cope with this rupture. I become afraid of abandonment, constantly waiting for the other shoe to drop in my relationship with Scott. While I desperately wanted to connect with my friends and fellow law students, I build protective walls around myself. I hope people will tear them down and force their way in, but on the outside I appear aloof and uninterested, so who's going to try? I tell myself I'm showing determination in the face of my new circumstances, but in truth I'm using hypervigilance and perfectionism to mask extreme soul loss. Not wanting to feel alone, vulnerable, or bad about myself, my addiction has the perfect petri dish in which to grow. Trauma has begun to do its work, disconnecting me from the truth of my own feelings, and from the essence of who I am. This rupture will help shape the next decade of my life.

Mom has moved in with Dan; my sister heads back to college; I go back to my apartment in the city, to start my second year of law school; and Dad goes home to our family house in Great Neck. There, he begins to take stock of his life. The *schmatta* business—a.k.a. the garment center, which has been the center of his working life—isn't what it used to be. I get a call from him one afternoon.

"I'm selling the house," he says matter-of-factly. "I'm having a garage sale, so you'll need to come out and take what you want."

Okayyyy, I think. *Weird.*

"Listen, I had to close my business. That is why I am selling the house. I can't help you with law school anymore."

"But you don't mean *this* year?" I start to panic. "I mean you're still paying for the apartment and helping me with my allowance, right?"

"No," he responds.

"What do you mean, *NO*? What am I supposed to do? Can't you help me, even just a little?"

"I'm sorry," he says, simply. "I really am, but no."

My whole life I'd grown up with the assurance that my father would take care of my education expenses. It was both implied and overtly spoken that I'd never have to think about making money, spending money, or where it all came from. This extremely privileged position was something I always took for granted. At twenty-two, I am of course old enough to figure it out—which I do—but it further waters the seeds of relational distrust that were planted a long time ago. While paying my own way teaches me independence and cements my can-do attitude, it also locks in the *no one is coming to help me* narrative that has been operating in the background since childhood. Too disconnected from my soul to self-soothe or find healthy coping mechanisms, this narrative gives me permission to blame others for the way I feel. It also gives me permission to reach for something to numb my feelings when they are too intense, finding solace in a boy or an alcoholic beverage.

When I pull up to my childhood home in the taxi, ready to collect my belongings, the driveway is full of cars. The garage sale is *happening*—as in, *right now*. Walking in the door I see all of our possessions laid out in the dining room.

"What the hell, Dad?" I demand when I find him. "You're selling the family photo albums? This dish I made at camp? My *jewelry*? You're not keeping anything?"

"No," he says. "Take what you want."

Freaking out, I start a pile—which quickly turns into boxes and boxes. As I pull my childhood out from under the noses of a bunch of bargain-hunting strangers, I can't stop shaking my head. *So everyone is in a different place in life now, fine. And Mom and Dad will probably never speak again. But we're still a family, right? We shouldn't be selling our past to the highest bidder, right?*

"There's no way all these boxes are going to fit in my tiny apartment," I say to Scott over the phone. "What should I do with all this stuff?"

"We can take it to my family's house," Scott says. After dropping the boxes in his parents' basement—where they will collect dust for the next ten years—Scott and I go back to the city and he drops me off at my studio apartment, still reeling. That week I get a job as a waitress at a Mexican restaurant— along with learning about torts, constitutional law, and criminal law, I'm memorizing the difference between a burrito, a taco, an enchilada, and a chile relleno. Scott's job at the law firm has relocated him to Austin for a case he's working on, so he spends most of the next two years commuting back and forth. While this forced separation probably keeps us together, it also means I have to sleep in the apartment alone—something I haven't done since my childhood home was burgled when I was six. I am terrified, and Scott knows it. One afternoon he calls from Texas.

"I got you something," he says. "You have to pick it up from the airport tomorrow at noon."

It turns out to be a Rottweiler puppy. I have never heard of a Rottweiler, but on the phone that night Scott explains that he will get a bit . . . bigger. Within a few months Tex is in fact bigger than I am. He takes up more room in that studio than either Scott or I could have anticipated. But I definitely feel safe.

Two years later, we are a makeshift family: me, Scott, and Tex living in a somewhat larger one-bedroom apartment in the city. With the trajectory we are on, the next step is to get engaged, move to the suburbs, practice law, and have kids. But to me, that seems like something "other people" do. Other people who, to my eyes, seem mostly miserable. Not me. I'm not even close to being done with exploring who I am.

Plus, after just a couple of months back in the same household, Scott's temper is starting to weigh on me. We've both grown up a lot while we've been living apart. And in spite of our bond, we've grown out of love. I am no longer able to push aside the fact that he has a short fuse. He's prone to yelling very loudly, and sometimes he'll punctuate his rant by breaking a dish or whatever else might be in reach. He never hurts me, but it's very unnerving. One afternoon, as Scott begins to lose his temper over who knows what, I watch Tex, my 120-pound fur baby, run behind me. *To hide from Daddy.* The future flashes before my eyes: if I stay, someday that will be my kid. That's all it takes. We are done.

Around that same time my sister calls. She's graduating from college and has been planning to move to LA with her best friend.

"Alice isn't coming with me to LA after all," she reports. "But I'm still going. You should come, too."

"Yes," I say. Just like that.

Looking back, I believe my sister intuitively knew that LA was the right place for me. But at the moment, I don't care where I'm going. All I know is that I need to get the *F* out of NYC and run toward something new and better.

CHAPTER THREE

Acknowledging the Trauma

I land in LA and feel lost. Specifically, I have no idea what I am going to do for work. I just quit being an attorney in New York and I have no plans to take the California State Bar, and I haven't figured out what I'm doing next. But I have to do something, since I have a limited amount of money saved and I need to start supporting myself—including buying a car. So to make money I get a job serving college kids at a sports bar. (And I'm drinking as much as I'm serving.) One evening when I'm "marrying" the ketchup bottles—the only thing I have ever married to this day—I have an epiphany. *What the hell am I doing? I'm a lawyer. I've passed the New York Bar. I can do anything I want in LA, why am I working here?* So like the starstruck girl from Long Island I am, I start interviewing in the entertainment industry. I find my way to one of the major talent agencies—International Creative Management, or ICM—and land an assistant job in the TV department. My boss is a young man, not yet thirty, named Andy.

Unlike so many infamous talent agents, Andy has no funny rules about how I get him his lunch or where his papers need to be on his desk. The only requirement to work for Andy is to be sitting in the chair across from his desk with a smile on my face. Enjoying myself with him. He's a man who loves his job. He ends every phone call the same way, whether he's speaking to his family, his coworkers, or a client: *Okay, thanks, love you, bye.* From across the hall I hear him yell, *Lunch time!* And I run and sit in the chair to help him decide where he should go to lunch. Sometimes his lunch plans would cancel last minute, and I'd get him takeout sushi. He always told me to get lunch for myself, too—a luxury I could not otherwise afford on an assistant's salary.

"Where are we going for your birthday?" he asks me, a few days before I turn twenty-six. "Um, I don't know?" I reply, caught off guard. While I would *love* for Andy to come to my birthday, I don't *expect* him to. I certainly don't expect him to *plan* the event with me. My sister just left LA for graduate school in New York City, and while it's definitely best for her, I feel her loss—especially as my birthday nears. But next thing I know, Andy and I are planning the whole evening. We decide on a dinner for ten of my friends, at a fancier sushi place than our typical lunchtime takeout. To my surprise and that of everyone there, Andy picks up the check for the whole table at the end of the night.

"Did you have the *best* time?" he always asks after one of these surprisingly generous occasions.

"Yes, thank you so much!" I reply, not knowing what else to say. He's only a couple of years older than me, and there's never been any sexual energy with him. Andy is like family—right down to handing me an extra twenty every so often, like a sweet older brother. As his assistant, I feel very taken care of. It's a familiar feeling: a man has shown up to help me navigate the tumultuous waters of my new life in LA. But Andy is also inspiring, and he makes me feel like I can really make it in Hollywood. When I watch him working, I am always learning.

The summer is rolling around, and soon it's going to be Andy's thirtieth birthday. Naturally, we begin to plan his party.

"Let's have it on the pier in Santa Monica and invite everyone," he says, his eyes dancing.

"What do you mean by 'everyone'?" I ask.

"*Everyone*," he says, with a wink.

The guest list has five hundred people on it. *I want everyone to have the best time*, he keeps saying. I will do everything in my power to make it so.

The night arrives, and I'm surrounded by celebrities and all the "important people" in Hollywood—most of whose voices I've heard on the phone but haven't met in person. I walk through the party in my inexpensive yet fancy outfit and think, *I want this, too*. Or, at least, I want what I *think* this party stands for: love, meaning, friendships, connection.

I love working for Andy, but I am also eager to get ahead. I'm not getting any younger. An opening comes up to be the assistant to the head of the television talent department, a woman named Kathryn. I interview for the position.

"You can have the job," Kathryn tells me. "But just so you know, Andy doesn't think you're ready for it."

Wait—what? How could Andy, of all people, ruin my big career-defining opportunity? My heart sinks. I feel confusion, mixed with betrayal, mixed with the old familiar refrain: *You are on your own. There is really no one here to help you.* I storm back to our floor and right into his office.

"I don't think you should work for Kathryn," Andy tells me in the calmest voice. "It's not the right fit for you."

"What do you mean?" I demand. "It's the obvious next step on the path to becoming a TV agent!"

"No," Andy says. "I don't see it. Also . . . Lisa, I am thinking of leaving ICM." I'm completely confused.

"What are you talking about, Andy? You love it here."

"CAA has been calling, and I think I might go," he explains.

"Well, then, I'm coming with you!"

"No, I don't think that's right for you either," he says, shaking his head. "I've been thinking about it, and I think UTA would be a better fit for you."

"I don't understand," I say, almost in tears. "You don't think I should get promoted here, but you don't want me to go with you to CAA. And now you're sending me to another agency?"

"Yes," says Andy, still perfectly calm. "Trust me, Lisa. I love you like a sister. It's really important to me that you listen. I'm going to CAA. You won't get promoted there soon enough. But UTA is more up and coming, there's more opportunity there."

"By myself?" I ask. "I have no idea where to start. How do I even get a job at UTA?"

"Don't worry! I'll help you," Andy says with a wink.

In the days that follow, Andy reaches out to a big TV agent at UTA and sets up an interview. A few days later I hear I've landed the job, and the plan is for me to start in February. But January comes and goes, and Andy has not yet left ICM to go to CAA. I remind him that my new job is starting February 1. He says I need to get permission to postpone my start date for two weeks.

"You can't leave until I do," he says. "Tell them you can't start yet."

"No, Andy," I say. "This is crazy. I agreed to start on the first. You're the one who told me to take this job in the first place. I'm ready, and I want to go. You need to hire someone or at least get a temporary assistant. But I'm starting at UTA on Monday."

And I do. I start work in the mailroom. It's a step down from the assistant desk I've been on for over a year, but I am okay with it. Andy assures me I will soon work my way up to an agent position at UTA. He's positive of it, and because of that, so am I.

After almost two weeks of being at UTA, Andy calls me on a Friday morning.

"Hi, honey, can you come to the office this weekend and help me organize everything?"

"Organize what, exactly?" As much as I love him, I am not pleased with this suggestion. "Andy, don't you have a new assistant?"

"I do," he says, with a smile in his voice. "But you already know everything, and she's just a temp. Please come this weekend? She can come, too, and we can organize the office so she knows where everything is and how to do everything."

"Fine," I tell him. No one wants to go to the office on the weekend, but Andy is one of my best friends. Two days later I arrive on Sunday morning to find Andy alone.

"Andy, where is the assistant? When is she coming?"

"Oh," he says offhandedly. "She can't come after all."

"Wait," I say, incredibly irritated. "I thought the whole point of this was to teach her how your office works?"

"It's okay, Lisa," Andy reassures me. "We won't be here long. I just want to reorganize the office so no matter who's working here, they can figure it out."

I begin and get to work. We listen to the latest Hootie & the Blowfish, each doing our own thing—me outside at the assistant desk, and him inside on the phone.

"Hang up the phone already!" I yell into his office, slightly annoyed. If I'm going to be here on a Sunday, he should at least be talking to me.

"One minute," he promises, covering the receiver. "I'm on the phone with my parents."

He finishes up and comes out to see what I've accomplished. I show him my amazing organizational system, which we both know won't last long since organization is actually not my strong suit. Hopefully his next assistant will create something much better.

"What did you do with the Christmas money I gave you?" Andy asks as we walk down to the parking garage together.

"I used it," I say.

"Did you buy the radio for your car like I told you to?" he asks.

"Um, *no*, Andy, I have a million bills to pay and no money and I need to eat so no, I did not buy the car radio," I say.

"I specifically gave you money to buy a radio for your car," he says. I can tell he's actually upset with me. "No one should be driving around in a car without a radio!"

My old Volkswagen Beetle convertible has holes in the floorboards and a horn that decides to beep of its own volition. I'm pretty sure a radio isn't the most important investment I could be making right now. But Andy is insistent.

"No buts, Lisa. You love when we listen to Barry White and jam out in the car. That's what I want for you when you are driving around." He almost seems to be pleading with me.

"Okay, okay!" I say, mostly to end the conversation. "I will get the car radio!"

"You promise?" he asks.

"Yes, I promise!" *Jeez*!

"Okay," he says. "Love you."

"Love you, too," I say, as I get into my car.

That night my conscience starts to creep in. That afternoon I'd snuck some charts out of the office—a breakdown of the names of all the people who worked at the networks and studios. This is before the Internet, so you can't just look up any old information on the web. I knew I would be on a desk soon at UTA—what if they didn't have a chart like this? But now I'm feeling nervous. Is it allowed to take a piece of ICM information into UTA? If someone finds out, will I get fired? I start to panic. Around 10 p.m., I pick up the phone to call Andy. I let it ring once and then hang up. *What the hell are you doing, Lisa?* I think. *It's time for bed and you're calling your ex-boss to ask him if you're allowed to bring a piece of paper to the office tomorrow?* I have that feeling I hate, the one of being insecure and vulnerable. *I will just ask him tomorrow,* I decide. Tomorrow, which is February 14, Valentine's Day.

When I wake up I feel a bit better. I take a shower and start blow-drying my hair. Back then phones were not surgically attached to our hips, so when I hear it ringing in the next room I decide to ignore it. But it keeps ringing. I look at the clock: 7:30 a.m. *Who the hell is calling me so early?* I put down the hairdryer and go pick up the phone. It's Luke, one of my other close friends in LA. We went to college together and have known each other for a long time. Luke is like another brother, my family in LA.

"Hey," he says. "Lisa, I'm so sorry."

My heart sinks. Did something happen to Scott? One too many bar fights, one too many motorcycle accidents.

"Sorry about what," I say, my voice shaking. "What are you sorry about?"

"You don't know?"

"Know *what*, Luke? What is it?"

"Shit," he says. "I'm coming over right now. Wait there."

"What is it, Luke? What is going on? Tell me *now*."

"No," he says. "I'm driving over. Don't go anywhere."

"*What is it?*" I demand, practically screaming.

Luke pauses, and then he literally whispers the words into the phone. "Andy died, Lisa," he says. "He committed suicide."

There is silence. Endless silence. My brain is trying to make sense of what is incomprehensible. But soon my body takes over. I hear myself screaming senselessly into the phone.

"Wait . . . *wait*! *Wait*! He could *not* . . . It couldn't . . . I just *saw* him . . . I have to go! I have to get over there . . . I have to see if he's okay. . . . I have to go . . . I have to get to him. . . ."

I hang up. Then I'm lying on the floor, sitting up just to catch my breath and throw up. In one of the worst moments of my life, I am braced against the front of my bed. I'm on the phone to New York, "Dad . . . Dad . . . *Dad . . .*" I don't know what I am saying, or what he is saying, but what I do know is he isn't coming to get me. Once again I have to fend for myself, neither parent coming to my rescue—neither one of them capable. Then Luke and some others are at my house and I'm sick to my stomach. Next flash, I'm alone in the apartment. I'm sitting on the floor and it's dark outside. I'm scared and alone. Then I'm panicking, running around the apartment screaming, crying, shivering, and shaking. I fall asleep, finally. I wake with a start in the morning, is it real? Did it happen? Was it a dream? *How am I supposed to deal with this all by myself? Where are the grown-ups?*

There is a knock at my door. I answer it and could not be more surprised. It's Jared, a client of Andy's whom I had become friendly with over the years. He lives in Santa Barbara. What is he doing here?

"Hi," he says. "I heard the news and I had to drive down. The thought of you being alone was horrible for me." How did he know I was alone? How did he know where I lived? Everything is a blur, but I am glad he is there. His company is a blessing. He sleeps on the couch.

The next days are a haze. I'm getting calls from his clients, colleagues, and family asking for more information. Why did he do it? Was he sick? Did he have depression? Was this planned? Had I had any idea he was going to do this? Were there any signs? I have no answers, only guilt, confusion. I can't stop replaying the call from Luke, and worse, the call

I'd made to Andy the night before it happened. I picture him in his apartment, hearing the phone ring. *If only I hadn't hung up, could I have saved him?*

Someone from ICM buys me a ticket back to New York for the funeral. I fly on the plane with Kim, another one of Andy's clients. They were very close, and I really look up to her. It's as if, one after the next, Andy's friends are carrying me through.

There is no service at the temple, only a gathering at the gravesite. It's mid-February in New York, there is a lot of snow on the ground, and I am in heels. I hadn't been to any funerals, and I hadn't known what to wear. I hadn't imagined we would be standing by a grave. Andy's close friends from LA are here: his best friend from ICM and others who would become my closest friends for years to come. All of us are broken by this loss. My feet are numb. I sit looking at them as the limo drives away from the gravesite. I wonder how long it will take until the feeling comes back. I wonder if my feet are black inside my shoes, frostbitten. My whole body feels black and numb. That feeling will continue for a long, long time to come. After the funeral and brief time sitting shiva, I return to Los Angeles alone.

THE WORLD LOOKS the same to everyone else, but for me it's completely changed. I'm constantly managing feelings of despair, loneliness, and isolation. I start to wonder if this was how Andy felt. How could I not have seen it? I replay his final hours and his last moments. Was he scared? Was he calm and resolved? I desperately want to ask him questions. I want to believe he's at peace. But I am not at peace: I feel as if I've been left behind, trapped in my own pain.

Unless you've previously experienced the suicide of someone close to you and really learn what to look for, the signs are not easy to see, if at all—especially for those closest. I go over every moment in my mind. I think of Andy talking to his parents on his last day, when we were organizing his office. I was listening to the conversation and to my ear it sounded so normal. Was he actually saying good-bye? Did he already know he was going to do it that night? Did he have bipolar disorder, depression? He was a drinker, but no worse than me. Did he have a drug problem I never saw? If so, how did he hide it so well? The questions never stop, and there are no answers.

Over the next few months my body starts erupting with the symptoms of PTSD. My anxiety skyrockets without warning. All it takes is an unexpected noise, or hearing Barry White on the radio, or someone saying the name of one of Andy's clients and I'm triggered. Suddenly it feels like I'm finding out for the first time that Andy died. My heart is pumping out of my chest, I can't catch my breath, and I feel light-headed—like I'll faint if I don't sit down quickly enough. Out of nowhere I'll break into a cold sweat, as if I'm about to be in real harm's way. But the terror is coming from within my own body and brain. It's my first experience of a panic attack.

I've never liked sleeping alone, but now I'm afraid to go to sleep at all. So I'm exhausted, under-resourced, and afraid of everything. I can't go a day without breaking down in tears. My life feels like an obstacle course now that I have to take detours whenever I'm out driving so I can avoid Wilshire Boulevard—too many memories of his house, the office, the restaurants we loved. I've developed an obsessive-compulsive disorder as a coping strategy, which has me checking every door, every window, and every curtain at least three times before getting into bed. I know it's irrational, but the urge to continue roaming the house wins out night after night. Everything has to be checked in threes: check each lock three times, each time opening and closing the door three times. Followed by the same madness with the windows.

The soul loss is coming at me from multiple angles. My relationship with my parents has been drastically different since the divorce. Mom is living in the city with Dan. She is off the benzos for now, and she seems truly happy in her relationship. But I cannot forgive her for what happened at the hospital. She put me in the position of being a mediator between my own parents, when only a few weeks prior I had begged her to admit she was having an affair and to tell Dad herself. I behave toward her as if I'm angry with her, when in reality I'm terrified at the loss of my mother figure and grieving my disconnect from her. Dad has begun a new career and is finding his way back to himself, but I can't get past the feelings of abandonment: leaving his children to handle Mom's psychosis, selling the house with no warning, and not coming to my rescue in LA after Andy's death. Neither parent is open to discussing what happened, so I'm left to bury the feelings. It is inevitable that now my body begins to become symptomatic, begging for me to attend to my psychological wounds. But still I do nothing, even with the alarm bells ringing. I don't know how to listen to my soul, so I suffer.

While I struggle with psychological and emotional pain every day, the thought never crosses my mind to see a therapist. On some level I'm worried that if I do, I'll end up in the psych ward—just like my mother. I try to go back to work at UTA but I am obviously a mess, a shadow of myself. While my only job is to deliver mail, everyone can see I am suffering. I keep getting phone calls from Andy's clients, colleagues, and friends. They're calling me in the mailroom and asking me what happened, what they can do for his family, how business decisions should be handled, and anything else they would have asked Andy himself. A past version of myself could have helped, but not now. The competent, informative assistant they had known me to be—whom I had known myself to be—is gone. My soul is wandering around looking for a place to just lie down, hoping to wake up to a completely different experience.

I am full of grief I don't know how to handle and too clueless to seek treatment of any sort. Yet, somehow I stumble into an experience that brings back a little bit of soul connection. Steven Spielberg, who—inspired by his own film, *Schindler's List*—has recently founded the USC Shoah Foundation to preserve Holocaust history. Seeing that I cannot make it through a day of work without breaking down, one of the partners at UTA suggests I take a medical leave of absence and go volunteer for the foundation. At the time, they are curating a visual history of the Holocaust, filming the testimony of survivors and witnesses. For most of the participants, this is the first, last, and only time they will ever tell their stories in full detail. So I volunteer. My only job is to hold the light while the cameraman tapes them telling their stories. It takes days, sometimes weeks to get through a single story. It's just the cameraman and myself traveling to the private homes of

SOULBRIETY

those to be interviewed. The cameraman and I bear witness to their deep and previously unspoken trauma, shame, horrors, and soul loss. I bear witness to story after story—tales of fierce determination to survive and the commitment to create postwar lives filled with meaning and purpose. I cry along with them, as I hold the camera light, grieving my own losses along with theirs. In the process, these brave men and women infuse me with hope and strength. I no longer feel alone with my despair. For the first time since Andy died, I dare to believe that healing will be possible for me, too.

CHAPTER FOUR

Breaking to Pieces

At the UCLA hospital I take the elevator upstairs and walk down the hallway until I reach the familiar set of double doors of the adolescent eating disorder unit. I'm there to see fifteen-year-old Frannie, who was rushed to the hospital after fainting this morning. The diagnosis is dehydration and malnourishment, as a result of not eating for three days. As the nurse comes out and greets me, I see she has a med student with her. I do a double take: it is Emily. She smiles and looks down, clearly not wanting to give too much away in her work environment. It's been ten years since her 5150 and here she is doing her psychiatric rotation in medical school. I'm so happy to see her, but I don't want to break confidentiality. The nurse and I discuss Frannie's case as she walks me toward the waiting room where Frannie's parents are waiting for me. Before we part, Emily speaks up.

"I would be happy to follow up with Frannie," she says. "I have some experience with the issues she's facing."

"That would be so helpful," I say, maintaining my professional distance for the benefit of the nurse. "Thank you so much."

I give Emily a wink as I walk into the small waiting room where Hilary and Robert—Frannie's mom and dad—are waiting. They've been doing Family-Based Treatment (FBT) for a few months. It's a type of eating disorder treatment that involves the parents taking control of Frannie's meal planning and prep and overseeing her while she eats the desired amount of food in order to get her back to a healthy weight. It seemed to be working well for a while; a few months ago she was doing better. She was at an appropriate weight, she seemed more engaged than she had in years, and she wasn't arguing with them as much. But suddenly it went downhill, and now their little girl is in the hospital. How did it take such a sharp turn for the worse?

This is exactly what her parents want to know. They want to know if I can "fix" the situation their daughter is in, and when they can bring her home. Knowing what I know about childhood trauma, I'm not sure going home is the best idea. I'm also keenly aware that I can't fix anything, and that Frannie has a long way to go to heal her eating disorder and what lies under it—the unhealed wounds that are driving her to starve herself potentially to death.

I explain that the family needs a new way of thinking about this situation. An eating disorder is a behavioral addiction, and just like any other addiction, there is always a reason why it started. But it is not just up to Frannie to recover. Frannie is not the *patient* of the family, I explain. Her disease is *part of* the family. Frannie is bringing into awareness something that has been bubbling under the surface of their entire family system, expressing the unhealed trauma that is inherent in all of them. From this perspective, everyone in the family needs to do work on their own underlying trauma to support Frannie's healing. Her parents need to look at their own family-of-origin issues and the invitations from their own souls that have gone unanswered for way too long. Only when they can see their parts in the crisis will they be able to separate their own feelings and triggers from Frannie's and actually be able to help. I talk about putting together a unique healing plan for everyone. This, I tell them, will be their Soulbriety "family plan."

Luckily for Frannie, her parents are up for it. I quickly learn that Hilary is not Frannie's biological mother. Robert had previously been married to Mary, who suffered from severe complications during Frannie's birth. She was in the hospital for the first six months of Frannie's life, and when she did return home, she was addicted to painkillers. She was a distant, inattentive, and quite disengaged mother. When Frannie was just two years old, Mary died of a drug overdose. Robert was of course devastated; he tells me he hadn't felt that kind of pain since his parents divorced when he was six. He says he was walking around in a fog of grief for over a year, and his sister took care of Frannie most of that time. Then he met Hilary, and they married soon thereafter. Since then, Hilary has raised Frannie as her own. From what her parents tell me, Frannie remembers nothing other than their loving and caring family unit.

Perhaps she doesn't have conscious memories of what came before, I tell them, but Frannie's *body* remembers. I ask how things are going in school and with her friends. I learn that her "friend" Chloe had taken a picture of her without her shirt on as a joke, and then sent it around to a bunch of kids at school. As a result they started calling her "flat Frannie." After the incident, the school made all the children apologize to Frannie and stop calling her names immediately. Pretty quickly the kids forgot all about it and things went back to normal, her parents report. But I know this is not true for Frannie's nervous system. She has at least three underlying adverse childhood experiences—a parent addicted to drugs, the death of a parent, and the loss of her grieving father who was unable to care for her—and now this new trauma on top. She may have appeared to "bounce back" on the outside, but it's no surprise there was something else happening internally.

A few hours later, I'm invited in to meet Frannie. I walk into her room alone and find her sitting up in bed, wearing a Justin Bieber concert T-shirt and sweatpants. She is coloring in a book and has a bunch of colored pencils scattered on the hospital side table next to her bed. There's a tube coming out of her nose, which is there to give her the nutrients she desperately needs. I also note a full plate of food on the bedside table, untouched. A nurse is stationed in the room 24/7, as Frannie is being monitored around the clock. The nurse is a young man, and from what's written on the whiteboard hanging over the desk, I can see his name is Adam.

"Hi, Adam, I'm Elisa," I say. "I'm working with Frannie's family and would like to speak to her alone if possible."

"I'm sorry," Adam says. "I can't leave her unattended."

I look at Frannie for her reaction. She sighs, looks at me, and rolls her eyes.

"Okay," I say. I pull up a chair and sit beside the bed.

"Hi, Frannie," I begin. "Your parents called me last night because they wanted some help. They're really scared and just want to make sure they're doing everything right to help you. Is it okay if I tell you a little about myself?"

She nods.

I begin to tell her who I am and what I do. I'm watching carefully for her reactions, noting when I see her connecting or relating to the stories I am telling about myself. This allows me to bypass Frannie's addiction and find my way in toward her soul. When I'm done, I ask how she's feeling.

"I want to go home," she says.

"I'm sure you do," I say. "It must be terrible being in here."

"I promise I will eat," she says. "Just help me go home. I will eat whatever my parents give me from now on. This was a mistake. I didn't mean for it to get like this—I just had a bad month with school and everything. I *promise* I will eat."

"Frannie, I'm not here to get you to eat," I say. "Let's stop talking about food. That's not the problem."

"What do you mean?" she asks, genuinely confused. "The whole reason I am here is because I didn't eat."

"Yes," I say. "But what interests me is something deeper. I'm more curious about *why* you aren't eating. Like, what feels so painful and sad and out of control in your life, that the only way to satiate yourself is by not eating?"

She looks right at me and begins to cry. Within seconds I watch her walls come down. As her vulnerability opens up, the veil to her soul gets thinner. I proceed with tenderness.

"Tell me," I say. "I'm right here. I'm with you and you're safe."

"I don't want to live like this," she confides, almost in a whisper.

When I ask what she means, she tells me she hates herself. She says that no one likes her. She feels ugly and fat and hates everything about her body. She just wants this feeling to go away. She knows she won't make it if she has to feel this pain every day for the rest of her life.

"Where is the pain?" I ask her.

"In my heart," she says.

"Do you think it might be in your soul, too?" I ask.

"Yes," she whispers, looking up at me. "Yes, exactly. But I can't reach it."

"I understand," I assure her. "I've felt like that too. There was a time I was in so much pain in my heart, and my soul felt so broken, that I started killing myself with drugs and alcohol. There were nights I went to sleep and I didn't care if I woke up the next day. But I figured out how to get better. And I want to help you do that, too."

"I don't know how," she says, the tears coming again.

"Well, what if I'm there to help you every step of the way?" I ask. "Because I think we really could heal some things, so you feel less pain in your heart and soul. I believe we can do it together. Would you be willing to give it a try?"

Frannie nods, and I relax. The soul healing can now begin.

———

AFTER THE SHOAH experience, I am no longer in a constant state of overwhelm. I'm able to come back to work at UTA. Soon I'm promoted to a junior agent position, and a new source of anxiety emerges: the pressures of my role. While I don't have any clients of my own yet, I'm assisting my previous boss with his clients, reading scripts that come in and writing coverage on them, and shadowing the agents who are responsible for covering Disney Studios so I can track and update the status on their projects. As the responsibility increases, so does my desire to explore the LA nightlife. One of the girls I start hanging out with is Tina. She's a bit more seasoned than I am, and one night she offers me cocaine. From that first bump, I'm hooked. It makes me feel in control, which means I can participate in any conversation and talk to the hottest guy in the room without an ounce of insecurity or anxiety. I realize that I've always loved being drunk, but the drinking itself I could take or leave. Cocaine I love, start to finish.

Tonight Tina is driving a group of us girls, and we're following a black Porsche up into the Hollywood Hills. The Porsche belongs to Nate, a successful talent manager who represents some very big movie stars. We ran into him at a Hollywood party, and we all ended up at a bar afterward. But in LA the bars close at 2 a.m., and if you aren't done partying—which we never are—you have to relocate to an underground after-hours club or go to someone's house. Tonight, Nate has given us the keys to his beautiful kingdom. As we pull into the driveway I catch a glimpse of the house: a modern mansion, with glass windows from floor to ceiling all across the front. We get out of the car and follow him inside, and the girls and I head for the living room while Nate goes into the kitchen. Seconds later he reemerges carrying a bottle of Kettle One in one hand and Jack Daniels in the other. Tina has already started cutting lines on the coffee table, and

I've found the stereo system and am getting the music going. Soon we each have a drink in hand and we're dancing around the living room.

After about an hour, I excuse myself to go to the bathroom. Nate tells me to go upstairs and use the one off the master bedroom because it's the nicest and the cleanest. I head upstairs, excited to see the rest of the house. In the master suite are more floor-to-ceiling windows, and the view is right out of a movie. The pool lights are on, the grounds are perfectly groomed, and beyond the yard the lights of Los Angeles can be seen for miles. I stand there for a minute taking it in before I head to the bathroom. Once there, I pull out my personal bag of coke. I always have one or two baggies on me, a secret stash that I have no intention of sharing. I'm beginning to hide my drug use from even my druggie friends, afraid even they will judge me. But I need more than they do; it just makes me feel better. I don't really think it's a big deal. I cut some lines on the marble countertop next to the sink, reveling in my personal party-within-a-party.

Before I leave, I fix my makeup and check Nate's medicine cabinets for any pills I might find interesting. I steal a Xanax, tuck it into my purse, and open the bathroom door—and am surprised to see Nate standing there.

"Oh hey," I say, nervous he knows what I was doing in the bathroom. "What's up? Sorry I took so long. I wasn't feeling great, you know, but I'm okay now." I start to head back to the door.

"Everyone else left," he tells me. I suddenly feel a flush of panic.

"What do you mean everyone left? Tina's my ride!" I say. "She wouldn't leave me here!"

"I told her I would take you home later," Nate says. An uncomfortable feeling starts rising up my body. It's a bad mix with the adrenaline rush of the cocaine, just hitting my system.

"Okay," I say. "Can you take me home now, then?"

"No," he says, and he starts taking off his clothes. I am frozen, completely stunned. He strips down to his boxers and walks toward his bed. "Come on, let's just fool around a bit then I will drive you home."

"I'm not really in the mood for that," I say, trying to keep my voice calm. Meanwhile I'm scanning the room for some way to escape. In a flash he's back up off the bed, and his face has turned angry.

"Take off your fucking clothes," he yells, stepping toward me. "We're going to fuck, and then I will take you home."

I don't know how I do it, but I manage to dart around him and out the bedroom door. I run downstairs and through the kitchen, where I see his car keys on the counter. Instinctively I grab them, run outside, and jump in the Porsche. He's following me, pulling on a T-shirt and screaming as I start the car.

"It's a stick shift! You can't drive it!" he yells, running toward the car.

Um, yes, I fucking can, I think to myself. Just then he jumps in the passenger seat. I am pulling out of the driveway.

"Fine," he says. "Drive yourself home."

We drive back to my apartment in silence. I'm so mad and too high to even realize how terrified I actually am. I can barely concentrate on driving, which clearly should be my priority given my state of mind.

I pull up at the corner of my block so he doesn't know exactly where I live and jump out. He gets out in his boxers and bare feet, coming around to the driver's seat.

"Hey, can I call you?" he yells as I run away.

I don't look back. The minute I get in the apartment I break down. As I start coming down from the high I realize what could have happened, and I'm terrified. Shaking, I pick up the phone and do what I always do: call Scott.

While Scott and I are no longer romantically involved, he has moved to LA to finish law school here. I still rely on him for emotional support. Whether we're in a relationship or not, he has always been there for me.

"It's me," I say when he answers. "Can you come over right now?"

"Why?" he asks groggily. It's 4 a.m., after all. "What's wrong?"

"Just come over," I urge, sobbing. "I will tell you everything. This guy tried to attack me tonight!"

"What? Are you okay?" he asks, fully awake now.

"Yes, I'm fine," I say. "I'm home now but I'm freaking out. Come over, we can watch a movie together until I fall asleep."

"No, Lisa," he says calmly. "I can't come over."

"What do you mean, you *can't*?" I ask. "Why not?" This is the first time I have ever gotten a *no* from Scott and I'm shocked.

"Because," he says, his voice lowering. "Carrie is here."

"Carrie?" I ask, confused. "Andy's sister Carrie?" I had introduced them a few months after Andy's death because she needed a place to leave Andy's dog. Since Scott already had

Tex, I thought he could handle another dog for a while. I definitely wasn't expecting *this*.

"Yes, *that* Carrie," he says.

"Scott, why would Carrie be there now? Are you *dating*?"

"Yes," Scott replies. I didn't care that he was dating someone, he'd dated a lot of different girls since we broke up. But Carrie? This felt too close.

"Please, Scott," I plead. "You know I don't care who you date at all. But not Carrie. Be with anyone in the whole world except for her. I can't have Andy's death be a part of my life forever, it's too painful. Please—please stop seeing her. For me."

"No," he says firmly. "I like her . . . a lot. I have to go." And with that, he hangs up. I know at that moment that he will marry her. Later he tells me that that was the moment he knew it, too. A year later, they get married. I'm not invited to the wedding, but Carrie sends me a VHS cassette—a video of the ceremony and reception. Likely to make sure I get the message that Scott is all hers now. I watch it with my roommate Joey drinking and laughing and making fun of everyone. But inside, my new reality is crystalizing for me: Everything has changed. There is nothing funny about the deep pain I am feeling. In that moment, another piece of me breaks.

At this point I feel like a boxer who's taking shots to the chin, stomach, and face, over and over again. Aside from the biological and psychological ramifications of the addiction I'm beginning to develop, my other problem—the one that will prove to be most serious, for years to come—is the loss of my own sense of self. The loss of my essence, the loss of my sparkle—the loss of my *soul*.

I TRY TO put my near-miss sexual assault behind me. I certainly don't connect it to my drug use, which only gets more out of control. It's now creeping into my late-afternoon routine. I am doing everything I can to keep it a secret, but I'm starting to get sloppy. One day at work, one of the kitchen staff brings over my little purse of coke and a razor and sets it on my desk.

"I think you dropped this in the bathroom," she says and walks away. Unable to acknowledge—even to myself—how insane it is that the *staff* knows what I'm doing, I just ignore her. When she is gone, I promptly put it back in my handbag. I make a mental note to be more careful. I don't yet have my own office, and my desk is in full view when anyone walks by. While I'm now allowed to set up auditions and negotiate small offers, I still have minimal contact with clients and I yearn for more responsibility. I need to focus if I'm going to prove I'm ready to be a real agent.

My house, which my friends refer to as "Fairfax and Hollywood" for the corner it sits on, is famous for late-night parties. It's the place you can always go back to after the bars close. On any given weekend night you might find a mixture of celebrities, rock stars, and randomers dancing to a DJ downstairs. The backyard is spacious, and we leave it open for party space and makeshift bars. When my thirtieth birthday approaches, Fairfax and Hollywood is the most obvious venue.

I'm as high as ever that night, and I won't remember much about the party the next day. But there's one moment I will never forget. I'm standing in the backyard, surrounded by over a hundred people, there for the occasion of my birthday. But here I am, all by myself. No one is talking to me, no one is checking on me. In that moment, I remember Andy's thirtieth birthday party. It had seemed like such an over-the-top success to me at the time. But standing here, drink in hand, hoping someone will take an interest in me at my own birthday party, I wonder if he felt lonely in that big room, too. Fortunately, the thought is transient. Someone walks by and hands me a shot, and I keep the party going for the next three years.

Soon thereafter I meet a new guy, Seth, when I am on a trip with a bunch of friends. He has big brown eyes and thinks I'm the life of the party. We don't live in the same city, so when we're together it's intense and wild. He lets me do my thing, and he enjoys the crazy fun nights I provide. For the first year, there's never a dull moment in our whirlwind romance. But after a while, he expects things to calm down—that *I* will calm down. Instead, my addiction is getting worse. I tell him not to overthink it, that he's making something out of nothing, that it's just the Hollywood lifestyle and he can't really understand, being the buttoned-up corporate Houston businessman he is. But in truth, I am disappearing. One night while I'm visiting him, I arrange for an early dinner with some girls I know in the area. I promise to be back at his apartment by 9 p.m. so we can enjoy some time together as well. Instead, after a few cocktails with my friends, the coke is summoning me. I dial up a different set of friends—ones I know will have coke on hand—and meet them at a bar downtown, intending on leaving after a few more drinks. But the coke and cocktails flow and the hours roll by. I stagger back to Seth's at 3 a.m. I'm unable to carry on a conversation so he lets me sleep, but when the morning comes he demands to know where I was. After some arguing, he accuses me of having been out with another guy. Since I had pulled this same stunt only a month before—when I left him at a party and disappeared for two hours—he wants answers. I'm not going to tell him the truth, that I was out on the street looking for drugs. It's no surprise he suspects I'm cheating on him. And in a way I *am* cheating—but not with another man.

One night almost two years into our relationship, he's had enough. I've flown in to see him, and halfway through the trip he tells me to leave. He says he doesn't believe anything I'm telling him. Rightfully so, given that most of it is lies. Lies to protect other lies, to maintain my dirty little secret. He also says he doesn't think I even love him, and he's right. I don't love myself, so I have no love to give. I take my suitcase down to the street, hail a taxi, and head back to LA.

A month later, I'm pretty sure I will never talk to Seth again. It's Friday, and usually I would be starting up a big weekend. Instead, I come home from work a bit early and take a long nap. I haven't been feeling well all day. I'm either hungover or actually sick—I can never tell these days. I have almost no awareness of my body, and little connection to how I feel inside. I walk down to the kitchen to get something to drink and run into Jill, my roommate.

"What's up with you," she says. "You look terrible. Rough night last night?"

"No," I say. "I just don't feel well. I'm really nauseous. I threw up this morning before work and haven't been able to shake it all day."

"Are you pregnant?" she asks.

"What?" I say, surprised. "No. I'm just sick."

"Are you sure?"

"Yes," I insist. But then I think about it. I mean, how can I be sure? I have no idea when I got my last period. Now that I'm thinking about it I don't think I've had one since I got home from Seth's.

"Shit, Lisa, you should take a test," she says, looking worried.

My head is spinning. This can't be it. I can't be *pregnant*. I can barely deal with the little things these days, let alone something so monumental.

We get in my car and drive over to Rite Aid. I come right home and run into the bathroom, take the kit out of the box, pee on the stick, and wait.

When I look down, I can't believe my eyes. *Pregnant*. Pure panic takes over. I'm spinning and have to sit down on the floor.

"I think I'm pregnant."

"You *think*?"

I show her the stick.

"But I have others," I say. "Should I do it again?"

"Yes," she says emphatically. She stands there next to me while I pee on two more sticks—both with the same result. *Pregnant*.

"I can't be pregnant," I say in between hysterical sobs. "I'm so scared."

"You need to try and calm down," Jill says. "My friend just had an abortion and she's okay now. I will walk through the whole process with you, you are not alone."

"What?" I just stare at her. I have no thoughts on abortion at the moment and no plan. I have no plan for anything in my life. I've been living moment to moment, every decision dictated by my drug use. I never think about anything but that anymore. I have no ability to comprehend what's happening. I just know I need to not be pregnant.

Jill, the acting adult in this situation, brings me into my room and we sit on the bed until I can catch my breath. She tells me I have to call Seth. I have to let him know what's going on. So I pick up the phone and dial.

"Seth?" I say. "Please don't hang up, it's important."

"What?" he says flatly.

"I'm pregnant." Silence. I don't know what else to say or to do. All I know for sure is that as soon as I get off this call I'm getting high.

"You're having an abortion, right?" he says, finally.

"Yes, of *course*," I say. Why is he even asking me that question—is it not obvious? I can barely take care of myself, much less another human.

"I will fly out tomorrow and be with you," he says and hangs up. He meets me at the doctor's office just before I go in for the procedure. He kisses me on the head and promises he will be there when I wake up. After it's over, I'm discharged into Seth's care.

"Do you want to go back to your house?" he asks.

"No," I say.

"How about we go sit on the beach for a little while?" he suggests. I nod.

We sit on the beach looking out at the water. I'm between his legs, with my back and head resting on his chest. We barely speak; there is nothing to say. Just as I wonder how he feels about this, I hear him crying behind me. I start to cry, too, but I have no idea why. Is it because my body hurts from what it's just been through? Is it because I love him and I have caused him so much pain? Does some part of me recognize that this moment will be imprinted on my soul forever? Or am I just feeling things I don't usually have to feel because I cover them over with drugs and alcohol? I don't know the answer to that question. But what I do know for sure is that the minute Seth drops me off at home, I'm getting high.

CHAPTER FIVE

Get Clarity

When I first meet Trixie she is wearing green velvet pants with green feathers at the hem, a tight black shirt, and a white feather boa around her neck. She has long black hair that's not freshly washed. She wears sunglasses and flashy jewelry and she smells like hard candy and vodka. She has no impulse control, she's manipulative and jealous, and she spins wickedly tall tales while promising me her lies are true. She is constantly coming up with grand plans and brilliant schemes at night, but in the light of day it's all nonsense and madness. Each day she attempts to walk through life gracefully but winds up tripping over herself. Looking back, what is most obvious to me about Trixie is not her out-of-control ego, but her low self-esteem. In order to rid herself of feeling unworthy, she is brash and bitchy. She lacks boundaries, which often leads to her being hurt and disappointed. Underneath her mask, I see her true emotions: sadness, anxiety, and shame.

I wonder who she really is and how long she will live, since she's constantly in danger, unable to think anything through. She's always chasing the next out-of-body experience she gets from drugs and alcohol. Trixie is so far removed from soul I am not sure I will ever be able to help her heal.

Trixie is not a client, a friend, or a family member. Trixie is *me*. Or rather, she's *part* of me. Trixie is the name I gave to my disease of addiction. But before I recognized and named Trixie, she still had many tricks and soul betrayals up her sleeve to drag me down even further.

—

'TIS THE NIGHT before the Oscars . . . and I am staying home. Or at least, I know that's what I *should* be doing. It's the first time I've officially been invited to the awards show, thanks to a nomination for one of my clients, a young movie star. I've known him since I started at UTA, when he was coming off a role in a cult classic film that had given him overnight fame. We'd been building his career slowly, trying to keep him from being pigeonholed in similar roles. I've worked hard to get him cast in other movies that allow his many talents to shine, and now the hard work has paid off—he's up for Best Supporting Actor. I couldn't be prouder or more excited for him—and for me.

The week before the Oscars is notoriously a nonstop preshow party, and I've already done my share of carousing. My addiction is going strong, but I still recognize that partying the night before the awards show is not a good idea. So I've told my friends I won't be joining them. Instead, I spend the evening pulling my outfit together: my fancy (borrowed) Vera

Wang dress, a matching pair of Gucci shoes and purse I get from a stylist friend. I confirm my hair and makeup appointment for the next day at noon, and I am just about finished with my preparations when the doorbell rings. It's a bunch of my agent friends stopping by to have a drink with me before they head to another exclusive party. *Just one drink . . . okay.* I have every intention of keeping it to one and really don't have a desire to go to the party with them. That is, until the drink is in me. At that point all of the planning, plotting, and promises to myself go straight out the window. Trixie is back in the driver's seat. One drink turns into a night of partying. Glass after glass of champagne, followed by its sexy counterpart, cocaine. Even when the party slows down and my friends head home for rest before the main event, Trixie is not finished. Which is classic: once I'm rolling, I never want the feeling to end. I never want to come down from the high, the energy, the escape. I can't bear the mundane, fearful, and sometimes painful thoughts of the sober day to follow.

My friends have now left without me, but no problem—I've found my "party crowd." We get a room upstairs at the hotel, to continue the party in a more private setting. As I sit in front of the glass coffee table with drugs and alcohol spread out all over it, I glance out the window and see the sun peeking over the horizon. There's nothing more beautiful than watching the sun come up in LA. But when you are coming down from the high and you've been partying all night, that sunlight feels as deadly as it would to a vampire stepping out into the blazing sun. I know I have to leave, as I can't bear the taxi ride home in any kind of real light.

As I get home at 5:30 a.m., I feel that familiar mix of shame, humiliation, and bewilderment lurking just inside the doorway. Unslept, still drunk and high, I do what anyone in my shoes would do: I order more coke. It's the only way to survive. I even convince myself it's a great idea—I'll just *stay* drunk and high! After all, two days up on coke is something I've done before. This is the magic of cocaine: master ideas just keep pouring in. What I do not factor in is that I'm going to the *Oscars*. Where I am expected to look glamorous, be social, and be working—all at the same time. I open a bottle of champagne just to begin to calm down.

When the hairstylist arrives I'm so jumpy I can barely sit still. It feels like it's taking her forever just to unpack all her equipment, and now she wants to chat with me about the *exact* style she was planning for my hair. Slow, annoying, and needy, I think. She's expecting too much from me. She wants me to take a shower, wash my hair, sit down while she dries it, and *then* fancy it up. How am I supposed to sit still for all of that? Another genius idea comes my way: Send the stylist home and cancel the makeup artist. I'll just brush my hair and freshen up my own makeup. I mean, it all looked great last night. It'll be fine.

I continue my one-woman pre-party as I wait for the limousine to arrive. It's worth noting that this car and driver is not in fact all mine; he picks me up and heads to pick up my client as well. We get to his house early, and the driver mentions we have about twenty minutes.

"Perfect!" I say. I decide to take a little coke nap—er, I mean *cat* nap—in the back before I go inside to greet him. After a while the driver stirs me awake, insisting I go inside. As I walk into the house, my client's hair and makeup team catch a glimpse of me. There hasn't been much for them to do on a guy in a tux, and I see the look they give me—and then each other. Together they offer to "fix me up a bit," as I must have gotten a little disheveled in the car on the way over.

Back in the car, I'm sitting between the client and another more senior male agent, on the way downtown. They're chatting away, but I'm having a conversation in my own head. How will I make it through the evening? Will the four baggies of cocaine in my borrowed Gucci purse be enough? I can hardly breathe, and I don't dare to speak. If I look anyone in the eye they're going to know something is off. So I concentrate on the plan: get across the red carpet, into the theater, and to the bathroom for a date with the white powder, credit card and the straw. Then, head straight for the bar to get a drink (or two) to take back to the table. *This is going to be okay*, I tell myself. *This plan will work.*

What I don't count on is the traffic, or the long line of limos ahead of us, waiting to pull up to the red carpet. I can hear the coke in my bag calling me, and I sit on my hands not to open my purse and sneak a bump. No one else seems to notice how long this is taking, and I'm not even half-listening to the celebratory conversation all around me. Finally we arrive. I basically jump out of the car and the first thing I see is the red carpet. The second thing I see is . . . *security.* The third thing I see—and to this day I don't know whether this was real or some sort of drug-induced, sleep-deprived psychosis— is the drug-sniffing dog. *Fuck.* I cannot get caught with coke in my purse, walking into the Oscars with a movie star. Not a good look, even for me. So before I know what I'm doing, I've palmed the baggies, pulled them out of my bag, and tossed them behind a bush—a fake bush, I should note, but I can't worry about that at a moment like this.

It will be okay, I tell myself. *There is alcohol waiting for me inside.*

Here is the thing they don't tell you: They do not serve alcohol at the Oscars. I discover this as soon as I get to our seats. It's nothing like the Golden Globes, where champagne flows at every table. The Oscars experience is as sober as it gets, you just sit in your seat freezing to death for five hours. I spend that time coming down, with nothing to soften the landing. For five straight hours I get stuck in a loop in my own head. *Why did I do this? How did I end up here? Will this ever stop? Will I ever be normal again?* Simultaneously another loop is playing: the voice of my addiction. *It's only a few more hours. There will be after-parties.* The rest of the evening is a blur. All I know for sure is that my client didn't win—but I was the biggest loser of the night.

———

THERE IS A moment in every addict's life when they know the jig is up. The Oscars is the beginning of the end for me; slapping me in the face with the reality of what I have become. I can no longer ignore that there is a widening gap between who I want to be, and who I become when I drink and use. I ruminate on embarrassment and self-recrimination in the weeks that follow the event. Slowly, an awareness starts to dawn in me. *I am powerless over drugs and alcohol.* Once I start drinking or using, I have no capacity to stop—even when the stakes are very, very high. Essentially I'm two different people: myself, and my addiction. I have no idea how to begin integrating the two, or how to stop letting the party girl take the wheel. Meanwhile, I am getting warnings from the external world. "If you don't straighten up we will fire you." "Since you never show up when you say, we are not inviting you anymore." "You don't tell me anything about what's going on for you, so I'm not going to share what's happening in my life either." "You have abandoned me as your friend and all you do is hurt me." *They don't understand,* I think to myself. *They can't comprehend the pain I'm in, because if they did they would be helping me not yelling at me.* But rather than empathy—or proposed solutions—I am met with closed doors, unanswered calls, and zero tolerance. I want to change, but I have no idea how. I am terrified and feel like I have nowhere to turn. I'm ashamed of my inability to manage my life, scared I'm destined to live this way forever. And below it all is the low hum of the more terrifying reality: if something doesn't change, I am going to die.

Six months later, one of my roommates from college is getting married. We're all going to New York City for a weekend that will include her bachelorette party on Friday night and a bridal shower brunch on Sunday morning. A bachelorette party is a huge problem for an addict like me. By now I recognize that even one drink leaves me vulnerable; it always opens the door into eighteen more, plus several bags of coke. So I make a promise to myself: *Absolutely no drinking on Friday night.* It works—at first. Somehow I make it through the pre-party without drinking, and I say no to wine at the dinner table. But alcohol has my full attention the whole time: I can tell you exactly what and how much everyone else is drinking. I'm aware of the one girl who keeps leaving the table to go to the bathroom—only to return with a sniffle I know all too well. Around 11 p.m. we head to the club. I have to hold on for just a few more hours. Around 2 a.m., my closest friends at the party start to leave and head home. It's the end of the night, and after hours of being "good"—with my addiction screaming in my ear to see what the coke girl was up to—I decide I can have *one* glass of champagne. One little glass. I totally deserve it; tonight has been a huge victory for me. My addict, now taking the wheel, is confident she can handle it. Look how well she's done so far! It's perfectly reasonable for me to enjoy myself for an hour.

Flash forward to Sunday morning around 5 a.m., when my Friday night is finally coming to an end. I've made it home to my sister's apartment, where I'm trying to get a couple hours of sleep before I have to get ready for the bridal shower. I've barely fallen asleep for an hour or two when my sister shakes me awake. I stink of alcohol and other peoples' cigarettes and have makeup smeared across my face. I'm a mess.

"Your friend Spencer is on the news," my sister tells me. "He's been in a horrible car accident." Spencer is an actor friend of mine; we've known each other since the beginning of my assistant days. Frantic, I run to the television. Fear rises up in me; if someone else I love dies, I will not survive. I hear a voice in my own mind, hissing, "You will not make it. If he dies, you will become a full-time drug addict." I am in a choke-hold of fear, facing my own future: the inevitable progression of my own disease of drinking and using. I'm triggered back into the trauma of Andy's death, and every other trauma that has come before or since. I'm frozen, crying, on the brink of a dark abyss.

Just then, I catch a glimpse of my six-month-old nephew. He's sitting on the floor beside me, surrounded by toys—but he's watching *me*. Witnessing his clear-eyed gaze, something inside of me wakes up. I'm flooded with a calm, clear energy. It's like a ray of light beams from his heart to mine, and I feel it is lifting me up out of the bottomless hole into which I've fallen. The longer we look at each other, the more grounded I feel. The world no longer feels like it's spinning out of control. I hear a new voice inside of my head, a loud voice, speaking with great conviction. "Get it together," it says. "You have to show up for him. You are not allowed to get worse, only better."

$=$

THE TEXT ON my phone reads, "Category red." It's my assistant at RMA, letting me know we have a client in crisis. We categorize emergency situations by color to communicate the level of gravity, and red means a lot of attention is needed, *right now*.

I excuse myself from the table—dinner out with the girls—and head to the bathroom where I call my assistant. She fills me in: we got a message from a random stranger, who says he has June—a longtime client of ours—with him. He found her sleeping in a car and knew she did not belong in this downtown neighborhood. He was concerned for her safety, and when he woke her up she told him to call us. I know

SOULBRIETY

immediately that she was there buying street drugs. I tell my assistant to call him back and thank him, get the address and let him know someone is on the way. We assign Chris to go meet her, and I call him to strategize. We decide that if she's still high or in trouble, he'll take her to the hospital. Otherwise I'll meet them back at her apartment.

I've been working with June on and off for the last eight years. When she first came to me, she was married to an extremely successful businessman, more than a decade older than she. Back then she was living a fancy life—always dressed impeccably, with a fresh blowout and manicured nails. She spent her time hosting charity events, buying art, and raising money for foster children—a cause near and dear to her heart due to her own childhood trauma and abandonment. With my help she'd succeeded in getting sober, but just months later her husband left her for an even younger woman. The humiliation and resurfacing feelings of abandonment were too much and she relapsed. In the intervening years we've gotten her back on track several times. But each time, things fall apart. After a short period of abstinence, she thinks her addiction is handled and the problem has been solved—so she stops working her Soulbriety plan. Relapse inevitably follows.

Chris arrives and lets me know she is coherent and sober enough; she's mostly just crying. Now that we know she does not require medical assistance, Chris grabs the keys to her car from the Good Samaritan and leaves his own car there. They head back to her apartment to drop off the car and meet me. I go back to the table and let the girls know what's happening. I grab my dessert to go, hug and kiss my friends, and head out into the night.

When I walk into June's apartment, she looks away. I can see she has a huge bruise on her face. Her right hand is all scraped up, bloody and bruised as well. Her face is gaunt, her eyes hollow. She begins to cry.

"June, what happened to your face?" I ask.

She starts telling the story—one I've heard before, of drugs, strangers, fighting, madness—talking a mile a minute. I'm trying to keep up with the story, but her retelling is blurry and disconnected, like listening to someone recounting a dream. The details are out of order and there is no throughline. As she rambles on I begin to make sense of the situation. The blister on the mouth; the burns on her fingers.

"June, stop talking for a minute," I interrupt. "What drugs have you been using?" June has always been a very honest addict, which is rare.

"Crack," she says. "And meth . . . and alcohol."

"Do you have any left?"

"No," she says. "That's why I came home. I need to sleep." I don't remind her that some random man found her sleeping in her car downtown, undoubtedly on her way to buy more drugs. Chris comes back into the living room and hands her a cup of coffee. She looks at it disdainfully and asks if she can have a drink instead. I tell her that if she agrees to go to treatment today—this will be her seventh time—she can have one drink. She agrees to treatment, but only if I let her drink until she gets there.

"I will do whatever you say," she says, "but please. I feel so sick." I can tell she is already having the shakes, and I know she will soon be safe in a medical detox facility so I reluctantly say okay.

"There is a bottle in my car," she says. "Can you please get it for me?" I say yes, but only if she gets in the shower while I'm going downstairs. She agrees.

The car is a wreck. There are clothes everywhere, strewn among the empty bottles of wine and empty baggies with white residue. It smells like cigarettes and spoiled food. I see a bottle with about half the wine still in it and grab it.

When I get back into the house she is still making her way to the bathroom. But immediately she grabs the bottle and takes a big swig. I walk into the bathroom with her to make sure she has no hidden drugs on her. She continues to drink as she gets undressed. As she turns to get into the shower, I see the bruising on her body. She looks away and hands me the bottle. As I shut the door, I hear loud sobs coming from the bathroom, but I keep walking into the kitchen. I pour the wine down the sink, tears streaming down my face. I stare out the window. All I can think about is how much she reminds me of Trixie.

———

I CREATED TRIXIE in an effort to protect myself from the shame and deceit of my using years, from the horrors "she" had seen. As I was trying to heal, I realized it was too hard to think of all those terrible experiences and choices I'd made as "mine." So I externalized them and imagined they had happened to someone other than me: Trixie. Trixie was separate from the sober version of myself I was so desperately trying to be, and creating her allowed me to put my past "over there" in my mind.

It was only much later in graduate school that I learned the importance of recognizing Trixie as separate from me and giving her a name. Without knowing it, I had been participating in a process that is key to reconnecting with soul: personification. Personification is the act of imagining three-dimensional personas for different, often contradictory parts of ourselves. It allows us access to pieces of our soul that have been cut off from our conscious awareness. Through active imagination, we gather up and bring home fragments of ourselves that have been lost along our journey, gaining a richer understanding of ourselves in the process. At the time, creating Trixie has a logistical purpose: my sobriety is more secure if I can keep an eye on my addiction from a distance. But there is a deeper, more meaningful process underway. Just as mythology allowed humans to formulate an understanding of our relationship to the world around us, personifying gives us additional knowledge about our inner world. If we aren't aware of the parts inside of us, they end up taking over—ruling our mood and personality—without our consent. We start to feel like someone else, like we're wearing a mask that obscures our real feelings, reactions, and behaviors. When you're being run by one of your parts, you may have a hard time recognizing yourself. In moments you might think, "I don't like who I've become." But at the same time, the mask feels like *part* of you, so you can't just take it off.

I often open the conversation about personification with my clients by asking them to remember the film *Night at the Museum*. In this movie, the statues in a history museum come alive each night, interacting with each other in positive and negative ways. I tell my clients to think of their psyche as the museum: filled with lots of personas that were created to protect us when we were young. Some are fighters, others are seductive, still others are quiet and invisible. They're all sort of frozen in place most of the time. But when we come across a trigger event that reminds us of a time in the past when we needed them, they immediately come to life and take over our adult capacity to reason. Since we created them during a traumatic or difficult time, they mostly behave in erratic ways. They try to protect us as best they can, but they don't have a ton of life experience that would have them make good choices. But once we're aware of these parts, we can see them as separate from the primary "self" we know ourselves to be. Then our self and the part can be in dialogue—we can actually learn from them and start to peacefully coexist.

Trixie has evolved and grown alongside me. She no longer wants me to do lines of coke with her, even if she's still impulsive and at times manipulative. But she also has a wisdom I've come to value. In dialoguing with her, I get to see things I might otherwise have missed; she draws my attention toward feelings and stuck places I wouldn't otherwise have noticed.

The purpose of soul work in general is to provide a pathway for us to reconnect to the aspects of our soul that have been sidelined due to trauma. There are many ways to go about this, from dreamwork to storytelling to art and music. But for me, personifying has been the most powerful path. Trixie was my first gateway back to connecting to soul; through her, I saw how certain parts of myself had been neglected, dismissed, and left behind. She acted out because she was in pain, and giving her a face and a name allowed me to feel compassion and understanding I wouldn't have otherwise been able to feel toward myself.

Naming Trixie is just the beginning of my process to create an inner world that is safe, nurturing, educational, and growth-promoting. As time goes by, I will name many other personas that will help me in different circumstances. I will learn to nurture and protect my youngest part, Short Pants. I will remember to turn down the volume when self-critical Gwen picks up the mic. And I will learn to relax and feel more secure by calling in my most competent part, Flossy. In this way, personifying is an easy way to make soul work more tangible and relational. Trixie, Short Pants, Gwen, Flossy, and the others are more than just names, they exist as unique images within my inner realm of soul. In distinguishing between them and me, I am able to draw on their wisdom as I grow down into the fullest version of who I am meant to be.

⸺

IT'S BEEN A few weeks since I last saw June, and she had her therapist call me and ask that I come see her. She's at a treatment center out of state, but I agree to go. I have such a long-standing relationship with her, and I can provide something the new clinical team cannot: continuity and a full history. I'll meet with June alone to start, and later we'll sit with her team and get on the same page. That way there is no splitting between what I say and what she retells them.

We meet in the cafeteria for lunch, and no sooner are we seated than she launches into a story of how well she is doing and how she never wants to go back to using. I have seen this kind of enthusiasm before, usually during or right after treatment—when willingness is high and temptations are low. But it's often ephemeral, so I shift the conversation.

"June, let's talk about why it may be hard for you to stay consistent with your recovery when you get out of here," I begin.

"Well," she says. "Maybe because my life is complicated? I mean between my boyfriend's bipolar disorder, not having enough money, and hearing my ex just had his third kid with his new millennial girlfriend. I know that's why I keep relapsing."

I shake my head *no*.

"That's not what I want to talk about," I say. "Those are the external circumstances. I want to talk about what's underneath your desire to use. I want to talk about your past." At this point in June's recovery, she can list her traumas like she's reciting the alphabet: her mom died in an airplane accident when she was thirteen. Her dad suffered from addiction and mental illness, so her aunt took her in and eventually adopted her. That meant moving to a new school and living with her two younger cousins, both of whom had behavior problems and so got most of her aunt's attention. And it meant being separated from her sister, who was sent to live with their grandparents.

"Yes, that is all true," I say cautiously. I go slow, since I know she's not going to want to go to the deeper place I am guiding her. Nobody does. "It's great that you can list all of these events; it says a lot about your recovery that you can recognize your trauma. But you already knew about all of these events before you went on this last bender. We have to unearth the *emotions* these events generated in you. Keeping the emotions buried is a defense mechanism that has been really important for your survival. But now that defense has to be switched off, I want to introduce soul into your recovery plan.

Otherwise the minute you hit a difficulty, you'll go looking for something to numb the pain again." Now I have her attention. "What do you mean, introduce soul into my recovery plan?" she asks.

"You rattled off to me what happened when you were younger," I explain. "When we experience traumatic events like these, we also experience soul loss. We have to turn off our emotions to make it through. But the problem is that once you turn down your emotions, everything else about you gets dialed down, too. Including your connection to your own essence, which is what I call your soul. We have to find a way to bring you back into connection with your soul, so it can guide you on the journey ahead."

"Sounds hippy-dippy," she says, rolling her eyes.

"Well, it's not," I say. "Soul cannot and more importantly *will not* be overlooked. I believe that parts of your soul have withdrawn, or descended out of your awareness. These parts, which have been too excruciating to even glimpse—let alone begin to heal—have been severed from the very essence of who you are. If you don't work to heal the rupture, you'll never stop reaching for alcohol when things get hard."

"Okay, but *how* do I reconnect to my soul?" she asks.

"It starts by voluntarily feeling your feelings. Consciously going into the memories that store sadness, anger, pain, and grief. It sounds counterintuitive, but when you go deeper into the feelings you'll actually start to feel more in control. When things get heated, you won't have to hide from the feelings by numbing out again. As we know, it's easy to stop using, but hard to *stay* stopped. I want to really focus on staying stopped and to give you tools to support you in doing so."

I begin to share about my inner world. I tell her about Trixie, Short Pants, and the other parts of me I've reunited with over the years. I can see a small flicker of light in June's eyes. I'm hoping personification gives her another way to understand what's happening to her, to reimagine her inner chaos in a more profound way.

"I want you to try and name the loud voices in your head," I instruct her. "Try to step back and really notice when your addiction starts talking to you, and name her. Name the young vulnerable part of you too. Then I want you to tell me about them next time we meet."

"Okay, I'll try," says June. "Then will you teach me how to get rid of the addiction part?"

"No," I smile. "That's the thing about our parts: they *are* us. Cutting off parts of ourselves is how the whole problem starts! But we can learn how to integrate their wisdom into our lives."

I go on. "Trixie never leaves me. She's always going to be here. But we live in harmony now, which allows me to appreciate her. I'm actually grateful for her now and view her as an ally. She helps me get closer and closer to my mission and purpose on the planet every day."

"Is this my new Soulbriety plan?"

"Yup," I say. "It's a really important part of it. Because unless we notice our wayward parts, name them, and differentiate them, they can just take over and cause all sorts of problems."

June looks a little confused, so I ask her if she's seen the movie *Night at the Museum*.

"Yeah, a while ago," she says. Then I see her eyes widen in recognition. "You mean I'm like the museum inside? I actually get that." I ask her to tell me about some parts of herself she can identify.

"Well," she says, "whenever someone of authority is speaking to me, I feel like I am this little girl again. Like I have no friends, and I'm on the playground, and the bigger kids are just making fun of me."

"Great!" I say. "Maybe we can meet her?"

"Yes, I think so," June says. "Actually, I think she's right here. She's crying. I think I'm going to name her Mandy."

"Beautiful!" I affirm. "What does Mandy want to say to us?" As June begins to relay Mandy's thoughts and feelings, I feel like I can finally relax. After all these years, June is finally starting to get it.

CHAPTER SIX

Gateways to Soul

The morning Spencer's accident is all over the news—
August 11, 2002—I decide I have a choice: keep drinking
and die, or listen to my soul and get sober. Thankfully, Spencer survives the accident—but I still choose the latter. I call
my therapist, Donald, and ask to come in for an immediate
session.

"Should I go to one of those meetings or something?"

"Yes, that could be helpful. Do you know anyone who can
take you?"

"Well, there is a woman I work with, and I know she goes.
I guess I can ask her," I say. "But I don't know, I'm Jewish and
nonpracticing. I hear it's pretty religious."

"You need just about all the help you can get right now,
don't you agree?" he asks kindly. "And the program is not religious, it's a spiritual program. Meetings are only a part of

it. Will you agree to go to one meeting before I see you next week?"

"Yes," I say.

A week later, I still haven't had a drink or any drugs but using is all I can think about. I'm trying my best to keep busy at work, then go straight home and not leave my room or bed for the night and get up and do it again the next day. This doesn't seem sustainable though.

Shit, I think. *My appointment with Donald is tomorrow and I still haven't asked the lady, Barbara, to take me to the meeting.* I head in to work that day with one goal. Get the courage to go talk to Barbara and make sure she takes me to a meeting *tonight*!

One o'clock rolls around and it's lunchtime. I see Barbara sitting alone in her office having a salad at her desk. I make my move.

"Hi, Barbara . . . can I come in? Or are you in the middle of something?" I ask, hoping she will tell me to go away.

"Not at all," she says. "Come on in, sit down. How are you, Lisa?"

"Fine," I say reflexively. "Well, actually not exactly fine. I mean *fine*, but . . . can I ask you a question?"

"Of course," she says, clearly interested in what the heck is going on with me. I can see her face has turned kind and her eyes seem more compassionate than usual.

"Can you take me to one of those meetings or whatever they are that you go to?"

A smile breaks across her face. "Of course!" she says. "I would love to. I've been waiting for you to ask."

"Wait, what?" I am confused. "How did you know?" She smiles again.

"You just know," she explains. "I could see the pain in your eyes one too many mornings. The meeting starts at 8 o'clock tonight, so let's grab a quick bite after work and go straight there. I'll drive."

Oh dear, this is happening way too fast and she has obviously been tracking my drug use. Did she talk to anyone else about this? Why am I going with her? Who is going to be there? I hope no one sees me there, I would be mortified.

"Awesome," I say, forcing a smile. "Thank you."

I'm barely present for the meeting. I know someone shares and we do some reading from a book, but I'm fully occupied with my one mission: staying as small as possible. I recognize a few people in the room, and I am terrified that someone will recognize me in return. At the end of the meeting a few people come up to me and introduce themselves. One of them gives me a paperback book with the words *Alcoholics Anonymous* embossed on the cover, the title barely noticeable unless you are looking for it. It's the book we were reading out of during the meeting. Another lady gives me a hug and welcomes me and gives me her phone number. Everyone is so friendly and nice, it makes me incredibly uncomfortable. I just want to get the hell out of there.

I go home and crawl into the safety of my bed and begin to read the book. I have since learned that most people do not read the book of Alcoholics Anonymous right away, but I am interested and I am kind of a student nerd. So I read for a while before falling asleep.

The next day I arrive at Donald's office. I sit down and immediately start to cry.

"Did you go?" he asks.

"Yes," I say. "It was okay, I can't remember much, it was hard to pay attention. I knew people there too. But then I went home and started to read the blue book they gave me."

"You mean the big book of Alcoholics Anonymous?" he asks.

"Yes, someone gave it to me before I left the meeting," I explain.

"How do you feel about that?" Donald asks.

"Relieved."

"Why?"

"Because I thought I was a crazy person," I say. "I thought something was really wrong with me and I was going to live the rest of my life that way. But maybe there is hope? I can just fix it and be done." Donald just smiles.

"So you're saying you identify as an alcoholic?" he asks.

"What does that even mean?" I ask.

"Meaning, at the meeting did you say, *Hi, my name is Lisa, and I am an alcoholic?*"

"What, are you *crazy?*" I ask. "No, I did *not* say that. I didn't say anything. I'm not there yet."

"I understand," says Donald. "Well, are you going to go again?"

"Yes," I say. "I made a plan with Barbara to go back Sunday night."

It takes me almost sixty days of sobriety and meetings before I'm ready to say I am an alcoholic. I knew I probably was one from the first meeting, but saying it out loud? That was another thing altogether.

OF THE MANY things I am shocked to discover in my first few months of sobriety is how much sugar alcohol has in it. As soon as I stop drinking I immediately start having cravings like never before. Specifically, I require chocolate-covered gummy bears on the daily. I drive every day to the ice-cream-slash-candy shop and get half a pound to take to work with me. At my desk I eat bear after bear. I almost can't believe I'm doing it, and I worry that I have traded one problem for another. But my new friends at the meeting tell me to cut myself a break. My only goal each day is not to drink or pick up a drug. Bears are harmless by comparison. But still, I am worried about my physical health. I decide to try going to "the gym," a place I've heard about on television and read about in magazines. I remembered meeting a woman named Cynthia at a party not too long ago, and that she was a personal trainer. Clearly I am going to need a trainer if I'm going to have the slightest chance of showing up at this gym place—let alone knowing what to do when I get there. So I ask the host of the party for Cynthia's number, and we agree to meet. First thing she does is a body-fat test. I've always been on the thinner side, so I'm shocked to hear that my body fat is so high I'm at risk for having a heart attack. *Jeez*, I think. *I'm only 33!* I quit the gummy bears cold turkey that day.

After about a month of seeing Cynthia three times a week, we are becoming more familiar. As I'm doing squats, struggling and complaining as usual, she asks me a question.

"So why did you decide to call me and begin to train?"

"I knew I needed to get in shape?" I say.

"But what prompted it?" she presses.

"Um, I don't know," I say, trying to figure out how much to share. I like Cynthia, so I decide to just tell her the truth. "To be honest, I recently stopped drinking and taking drugs." I am not ready to call myself an alcoholic or drug addict yet, but I am starting to get used to talking about my sobriety.

"Wow, that's amazing," Cynthia says. "How long are you sober?"

"Thirty-two days," I say proudly.

"I'm eighteen years sober," she says. I stop the squats and look at her.

"Really?" I ask, in disbelief. "I had no idea!"

"Yup," she says. "Keep squatting."

"But you were at that dinner party," I say between huffs and puffs. "We were all out-of-our-minds drunk!"

"No," she laughs. "*You* were out-of-your-mind drunk. I was sober and sitting next to you, wondering if you knew you'd probably need to get sober one day."

"That's amazing," I say. "I knew I liked you, but it's so random that I called you."

"Not really," she explains. "It's what we call a God Shot—a serendipitous encounter or coincidence that happens at the exact moment you need it. Do you have a sponsor?"

"No," I say. "I'm not sure I'm ready for that yet."

"Well, I could be your temporary sponsor," she offers. "Until you feel ready for someone more permanent to do the steps with you."

And with that, I have my first sponsor—another angel who helps save my life.

I love Cynthia and quickly come to trust her with my deepest secrets. For example, I confide in her that I'm starting to notice I'm really uncomfortable creating authentic relationships with other women now that I am sober. I don't feel I can be vulnerable with women now that I am so raw. Much later, I will realize this discomfort is a symptom of the traumatic and anxious relationship I had with my own mother. But Cynthia isn't thinking about healing my trauma. Her solution? Take me to her favorite gay women's meetings and instruct me to share about how much I don't like women. I summon the courage to do so, and I get bombarded by hugs and love the minute the meeting is over. The love they shower on me in these meetings teaches me I can trust females and helps me get comfortable with feminine strength. For the first time in a very long time, I feel safe being vulnerable in front of other women.

It's soon clear that Cynthia is not just my "temporary" sponsor—so she tells me it's time to do the steps. I take my time to carefully understand the first three and arrive at the fourth step. This is the moment where you write down all the resentments you're hanging onto, toward both others and yourself. After listing the experiences that have made me resentful, Cynthia tells me to write down which of my character defects were on display in each incident. Soon I am staring at a repeating list: fear, insecurity, jealousy, denial, arrogance, dishonesty, and selfishness—just to name a few. When I finish the inventory, Cynthia and I meet at the beach to watch the sunset while I complete the fifth step: reading the whole list out loud to her. Unfortunately, before I'm halfway through we are interrupted by a police officer, telling us the beach is closed for the night. So we make a plan to meet in the same spot the next morning. Not wanting me to sit with this chronicle of pain overnight, Cynthia takes the pages of resentments and character defects with her and we say good night.

The next morning when we meet up at the beach, Cynthia has a funny look on her face.

"What's wrong?" I ask.

"Nothing," she says. "But I want to talk to you about resilience in sobriety."

"Okay . . . ?" I have no idea what she means, but I trust her. If I need this important lesson before I finish reading my humiliating list of secrets, I'm here for it.

"Yesterday I had to return my rental car," Cynthia begins. "And by accident, I left your pages on the front seat of the car."

I stare at her. Suddenly my mother's advice comes flooding back: *Never write anything down you wouldn't want others to read.* I begin to cry.

"So you mean everyone at Avis is reading about my life?" I say between tears.

"No," she says. Hopefully, I look up at her. "It was Hertz."

I can't help but laugh, but I still feel gutted. Cynthia assures me that most people only care about themselves, and the pages most likely got thrown away immediately.

"It's only you who believes in the power of those past experiences," she says, wisely. "So, are you willing to let them go? Are you willing to work on the character defects you saw in yourself and develop your self-worth—beginning with your courage, determination, humility, grace, and resilience?"

"Yes, I am," I say. "Let's do it."

I have been working on deepening these assets every day since then.

ONCE I'M SOBER, I have to be creative as I navigate all the after-hours screenings, parties, and client dinners that are expected in my line of work. I am lucky to have found a good crew of sober friends, male and female, and I do my best to stick with them for personal socializing. But at work events, I'm on my own. I talk to both Cynthia and Donald before each event, and they say the same things: drive your own car, make a plan for when you'll leave and then stick to it, and remember that nothing good happens after 11 p.m.

The hardest part is the first twenty minutes of an event. It takes about that long for me to get comfortable in my new surroundings. Back when I was drinking I had a routine: head straight to the bar, down my first drink and have my second in hand within the first ten minutes. Now I develop a new routine. Upon entering a party, I walk straight to the bathroom instead of the bar. I calmly collect myself in the stall and practice my breathing. Then I say a little prayer, usually the Serenity Prayer: *God, grant me the serenity to accept the things I cannot change, the courage to change the things I can, and the wisdom to know the difference.* After a few minutes, I head back into the party. Next, I go to the bar and order myself a Diet Coke. One night I accidently get a Jack and Coke instead. I literally spit the drink out onto the floor and switch to water from then on.

After getting my drink, I find someone who seems easy to talk to. I stay away from real work conversations to begin with. All I can handle at this point in the night is some light *hi, how are you.* If for some reason I can't find a gentle soul to chat with and I get anxious, I just head back to the bathroom and start again. Stall, breathe, pray—leave my drink in the bathroom and go to the bar to get a new one. By this point it's usually been twenty minutes or so. I'm getting used to my fish-out-of-water surroundings, and I'm ready to network—which is the whole reason I'm there. I do what I need to do, leave between 9 and 10 p.m., and I'm home in bed before 11 p.m. every time—no exceptions.

=

ONE CHRISTMAS VACATION, I travel with a few friends to Sydney, Australia. I've been on a few sober vacations at this point, and since there's another girl in our group who isn't drinking, I think it will be fine. Off I go—halfway around the world.

One night we meet a bunch of Aussies out on the town, and a few of the guys invite us out on their boat the next day. We meet up at 10 a.m., super excited to hang with our new friends, sunbathe on the water, and see the coast from the ocean point of view. Everyone is so nice, and the boat is gorgeous. We head out to sea, and once we're so far out we can't see shore anymore, the boat slows to a stop so we can all hop in for a swim. I am in *love* with Australia! As I'm climbing back onto the boat after my dip, I see everyone gathered around the table. Food! I'm so happy, I'm starving after the swim. But as I get closer to the table, I see it's not food they're enjoying—the table is crisscrossed with lines of cocaine, surrounded by flutes of champagne, bubbling in the sunlight. *Champagne and cocaine, my two favorite things in the world.* My mouth starts to water and my heart begins to beat fast. I quickly relocate to the other end of the boat, sit down, and contemplate my next move. One voice in my head says, *You only have two years sober. It wouldn't be the end of the world to start over. This is a once-in-a-lifetime event, and it's your favorite! Plus there's nothing else to do—you're here on the boat in the middle of the ocean. Just enjoy yourself.* Thankfully, another voice butts into the conversation. *Call Peter!* it says. *NOW!* Peter is a sober friend from LA who—in another well-timed God Shot—happens to be in Sydney right now for work. *Get your phone and call him now!* I do what the voice says.

"Peter, *help!*" I say, as soon as he picks up. "I'm on a boat in the middle of the ocean with some guys we met last night. And they just took out a ton of blow and six bottles of champagne."

"At 11:30 a.m.?" Peter asks.

"That's what *I* thought!" I concur. "But what do I do?" I'm now panicking, and my impulsive reptilian brain has taken over. I can think of nothing but my two longtime friends, calling me from the table across the boat.

"Tell them you want to get off the boat," he says.

"What do you mean?" I ask, genuinely perplexed. It has not occurred to me that getting off the boat is an option.

"Just tell them you want to get off the boat!" he says, as if it were the most obvious thing in the world. Suddenly my rational brain comes back online.

"Genius!" I yell into the phone. Hanging up I start shouting, *I want to get off the boat!* I keep yelling until finally someone asks, "Why, are you okay?"

"No, I'm not okay," I say. "*I want to get off the boat.*" I just keep saying the same thing over and over again, afraid to move from the seat I am in. Finally my two girlfriends come find me. I tell them they need to get the guys to take me to shore. They agree but explain that we are now hours from the original town where we left; if they take me straight to shore I'll have a long bus ride back to the hotel.

"No problem," I say. "I want to get off the boat." My friend Sideny agrees to come with me. We sit on a clunky bus with no air conditioning and travel two-and-a-half hours back to the hotel. I have never been so happy in my whole life. *I'd done it.* But I haven't done it alone. Had I not reached out to Peter, I would be having a very different day—and maybe a different life—ahead of me.

———

I AM FINALLY in my groove at work. Now sober, my mind is sharp again and my creative juices are flowing. I get up early, work out regularly with Cynthia, and I'm really starting to make things happen at work. One day I get a call from my financial planner.

"Lisa, something weird is going on," he says. "You have about ten credit cards with your name on them that are not yours."

"That's weird," I say. "Did someone steal my identity?"

"Um, yes," he says, hesitating. "But that's not the weird part."

"Oh?"

"The weird part is that the bills for all the cards are going to the same address, and the minimum payment is being made each month."

"What?" I ask. "Why would someone make payments on stolen credit cards?"

"Well, it makes more sense if you know the address they're going to," he says.

"Okay, what's the address?"

He repeats an address that I know very well.

Mom.

I've been sober for two years, and my mom—now separated from Dan—is living in NYC alone. Since I've been sober I've had a really hard time connecting with her. I know something is off, but I don't know what. (I've found in the years since that it's hardest to see early signs of addiction in our own family.) I know she's struggling financially, and I've been paying for her apartment and most of her bills for months now. So this revelation is quite shocking: *Mom stole my identity, but at least she's trying to be polite about it.*

I haven't seen her in person for a long time, and I even have a hard time speaking to her on the phone. She sounds somewhere between a little off and for sure high. Clearly I have ignored the problem for too long. I call my sister. After she fills me in with a ton more information that I had not known because I was preoccupied with my own addiction, we agree to intervene. With only two years of sobriety myself, we send our mom off to rehab for the first time. She's in her late sixties.

After two weeks, I make the drive to Palm Springs to see her for her first visiting day. I'm waiting in the lobby when she comes bouncing in. The last time I had seen her, the day we sent her to treatment, she'd been falling apart. A tiny eighty-five pounds, she had pills coming out of every tissue, pocket, and handbag in the house. As the driver we'd hired pulled away down the street, my sister and I had looked at each other with tears running down our faces. We were still unsure if the decision to send her to treatment was the right one. But today, this bubbly lady walks in with a lightness in her step. She's smiling and gives me a big hug. I literally do not think I've ever met this woman before. We walk outside and get lunch.

She tells me all about her roommate, the people she's meeting, and the stories she's heard.

"I love it here," she says. "I was mad and scared at first, but I'm really grateful you sent me here!"

As I drive away, I'm marveling. I wouldn't have believed it was possible a few weeks prior. I feel so grateful. Not only has my sobriety given me *my* life back, but it's given me the opportunity to have my mom back, too.

CHAPTER SEVEN

Facing Dark Nights

M y new client Ricky is an NBA star. He's been sober for over a decade, but recently he's gone back to drinking. The night I get my first call from his family, he's just had a car accident. No one is hurt, thank god, but he's gotten a DUI and the press is about to pick up the story. Even more importantly, Ricky is a complete mess. He needs to get into treatment immediately. I get in my car and head over to his house, where his wife and manager are waiting for me.

"So, tell me everything," I say. They are more than happy to oblige. They want—*need*—to be heard. Each has different concerns and fears. Meanwhile, Ricky is drinking in the next room. He's not quite ready for me yet.

When Ricky's wife and manager are done giving me the download, I ask if they are open for feedback. This is a technique I learned early on in my sober days, and it has served me well as a crisis manager. *When you have something to say that may be hard to hear, ask for permission first.* If you don't, the minute you start speaking, defenses are liable to go up. By gently asking for permission, you circumvent that pattern. When someone has invited you to speak, they're more likely to listen with an open heart.

Upon receiving their permission, I start talking. First, I explain what I do, followed by my preliminary assessment of Ricky's situation. Once I have everyone's full attention, I tell them I need to speak to Ricky's attorney. Often I'm the one recommending an attorney—one I know will answer the phone at midnight—but in this case they already have one. We must make sure it's okay for Ricky to leave the state for treatment. I learned this the hard way, early in my intervention days. I had a client on the verge of death from his addiction. He was also on parole. I took my chances and booked him in the best treatment facility I knew . . . which was several states away. I never heard the end of it from the most prominent criminal attorney I knew.

"Try *not* to do that again, Elisa," she said, in a voice that let me know I would face my own consequences if I did. The law is not always on the side of mental health, I've discovered. Sometimes it makes saving lives a bit more difficult than it needs to be. Hopefully one day that can change.

Ricky is cleared, so I begin to discuss his treatment options. There are many considerations when deciding where to send someone for treatment. First, I need to determine whether they will need medical care; that is, if they're going to be detoxing, alcohol and benzodiazepines are the most dangerous to detox from and require medical attention. I also need to determine whether they need to be in psychiatric care if they're experiencing psychosis or they are a harm to themselves or others. If we're sending someone directly to residential treatment, I need to know all the underlying issues—what we are treating them for. It's a long conversation.

After going through all the particulars with Ricky's team, we decide on a treatment center that has both substance- and trauma-focused care. I have the office charter a flight while I break the news to Ricky.

Ricky's wife goes and gets him, and he walks into the room looking like a little kid who's in big trouble. He sits on the couch next to me, and the next thing I know he's sobbing openly. He is so ashamed, he tells me. The alcoholism is so at odds with who he knows himself to be on the inside.

"Has anyone ever explained the disease of alcoholism to you?" I ask him. "I mean, how the brain actually works?" He shakes his head no. I ask if he can handle neuroscience 101, and he nods his head. "We have two parts to our brain," I start. "There's the back part of our brain, our reptilian brain. It's responsible for our heartbeat, our body temperature, and other things we do not need to worry about or control. Its job is to keep us alive at all costs—so it's home to our fight, flight, or freeze mechanism. Then there's the front part of our brain. It's where rational thinking, decision-making capabilities, impulse control, and other functions that are under our control reside.

"In a healthy, normal brain, these two parts work together. Let's say you run into a bear in the woods. You need to act before you can think. So the reptilian brain swings into action, and you hit the dirt and play dead. A few minutes later the bear has wandered off, and the frontal cortex comes back online. It sends a message to the reptilian brain that it's safe to crawl away." Ricky nods his understanding; he's really listening.

"Here is the key," I continue slowly. "With the disease of addiction, the handoff between the front and back brains ceases to work properly. Your reptilian brain experiences alcohol as a survival-level need. It will stop at nothing to get more. And it hijacks your rational frontal cortex, not allowing it to come back online and make a reasoned decision to stop."

I can tell Ricky is hearing the heart of my message. *No matter what, once you started drinking again, you were destined to fall back into the cycle.* For some, the descent takes longer. For others, the downward spiral starts right away. But all alcoholics and addicts who start up again are on borrowed time. Soon, the "yets" creep in: I haven't been arrested . . . *yet.* I haven't had a DUI . . . *yet.* I haven't lost my job . . . *yet.* I haven't lost my kids . . . *yet.* Is this a way to live? Maybe, if basic survival is all you're after. But if you are looking to thrive? Then deep work—soul-level work—is needed. And for the soul work to take hold, abstinence is required.

Ricky wants to thrive, he tells me. So he agrees to go to treatment. I tell him about the center I want him to go to and that it's a few states away. He's terrified, but he also sees the pain on his wife's face. My words are sinking in, and he's starting to see me as an ally.

"So we will leave later this week?" he asks.

"No," I reply. "We are leaving now. There's a private plane waiting at the airport."

"Wait," he says, looking panicked. The shock is understandable; this is all happening very fast. I can see past trauma and fear creeping in. His body language shifts, and his eyes are laser focused on me now. "What about practice?"

"I spoke to your attorney," I tell him. "You are okay to leave and go to treatment. It's what's best for you right now." After a few minutes he's adjusted to the new reality. He's ready. He says good-bye to his wife, and just a couple of hours later we're sitting next to one another on the plane. I can feel the pain, shame, and fear seeping out of every pore of him. We land, and as we taxi I turn on my phone. I want to make sure the treatment facility staff is waiting for us at the airport as planned. And there it is on my newsfeed: Ricky is facing suspension from the team.

I watch as he slowly looks at his own phone. I see whatever color he had left in his face draining out. He looks at me.

"What am I going to do?" he asks quietly. "Playing basketball is what I do."

I look him straight in the eyes. "Do this work on yourself, get sober, and not only will you play again but you will gain so much more from life."

I know Ricky needs a course correction. I know he needs to feed his soul in other ways, and this will be an opportunity for him to grow down and create more meaning and purpose than he ever dreamed.

He takes a deep breath and stands up. I watch as he walks down the stairs and out onto the dark tarmac—toward the next step on his soul's journey.

—

THREE YEARS AFTER I get sober, the movie *Wedding Crashers* debuts—a movie I put together from start to finish. It's a blockbuster hit, and its two stars, Vince Vaughn and Owen

Wilson, are the toast of Hollywood. Their agent, Lisa Hall-erman, is a big deal, too. I'm getting phone calls every day from the Hollywood elite, CEOs of Fortune 500 companies, and other Very Important People. Everyone wants to get into business with the biggest movie stars of the moment. It's never been so easy to court clients away from other agencies. I'm on the phone all day, promising actors the moon. *I did it for Vince, didn't I?* I assure them. The attention is intoxicating. Like any other addiction, it's rearranging me from the inside out. I begin to believe I am the mask I'm wearing. *I'm Lisa Hallerman.* I dress accordingly, using Barneys—conveniently located directly across the street from UTA—as my *Devil Wears Prada* closet. Little black dresses that cost a *lot.* Power suits. And of course, the high heels with the red soles.

It's a far cry from the style I had when I was drinking and using—which was Trixie-style, *Look at me!* Bright colors, lots of skin showing and—because I was already high before I left the house—that "looks good when you're blurry drunk" look. After I got sober, my style desperately needed to change, but I had no idea what to change it to. I still didn't know who I was or what I liked, so I would take little pieces of other people and make them my own. I would put something on and ask myself, *Would Nicole Kidman wear this?* If the answer was no, I would change. No longer wanting to be the center of attention, I would sit at dinner parties trying to figure out how to participate without a drink in my hand. I'd ask myself, *Do I need to be speaking right now?* If the answer was no, I'd concentrate on sitting quietly and enjoying other people's stories. Once, just after getting sober, I was driving my Alfa Romeo in Santa Monica. This had been my dream car when I was using; you could still see coke dust cemented in the seat fabric. Just then I passed a girl with her blonde hair blowing out the window of her giant black SUV, upbeat music blasting. To me, she looked amazing, happy, and free—not a care in the world. So I dyed my hair blonde (*blonde* blonde) and traded in my Alfa Romeo for a black Cadillac Escalade. But a few years later I have evolved into a serious badass.

A first look at a secret script . . . a meeting with the "it" director . . . lunch with the chairman of a studio . . . invitations to all the parties . . . a primo table at a fully booked restaurant . . . everything I had ever asked for, I get. Overnight I've gone from hanging out with dudes in dive bars to walking red carpets around the world. When people ask me, *What's next?* I think, *What else? More money, more fame, more of this ego high, please.* But as my ego is expanding, so is the resentment around me.

The emotional abuse one can experience in Hollywood can be overt or subtle—and I have seen it all. My first taste happened on my very first day as a temporary assistant on an agent's desk. Let's call him Mr. I'm-an-asshole-and-so-insecure-I-must-pick-on-you-to-feel-okay. (Or Mr. I, for short.) Mr. I is standing in the hallway with a colleague, talking about what they're going to do that night. I'm trying to expertly answer Mr. I's phone: catch every call, say exactly the right thing, say and spell the caller's name correctly without asking, and politely get them to *please hold* while I see if Mr. I is available.

Out of the blue, Mr. I turns away from his conversation and literally *screams* at me, *"Get me the calendar!"*

I'm a few inches away from him and so startled I am frozen to my seat. Thankfully my frontal brain jumps back online quickly. *The calendar?* I ask myself. *Does he want me to get up out of this chair and walk into his office and get him his datebook? Does that mean he wants me to leave THE PHONE?*

"*The calendar from my office!*" he yells again. Okay, got it. He *does* want me to get up. I go into his office and retrieve his black Filofax. I hand it to him and turn back to my desk. Before I can sit down, he throws it at me. I'm shocked as he starts laughing, then screaming to anyone who will listen, "Not *my* calendar. The Calendar Section of the newspaper!" I stare at him. Is this normal behavior? Is this allowed? I mean, I used to work at a New York City law firm and appear in court every day and I never got screamed at like this. I want to scream back at him, *I just fucking moved here, you moron, and I had no idea about the Calendar Section of the* LA Times *because I read the* New York Fucking Times *like any intelligent person.* But I don't.

I am taught early in my Hollywood tenure when to mute my voice this way. Not long after the Calendar incident, I'm interviewing for a new desk. As I sit down, the hiring agent looks at me curiously.

"You look familiar," he says. "Did we fuck?"

I think all young women in Hollywood imagine that with success, power, and "importance," we will eventually earn our place. That our voices will be welcomed, that finally people will listen to us. *Not so fast.* Instead we can face years of snickering, lewd comments, disgusting attitudes, and resentment at having to work for or with a *woman*. Sometimes the men are more subtle—it's an eye roll, or feet on the table when the women are sitting properly in our skirts and heels, or getting up and walking around the room exactly when the only woman at the table is speaking. Over time this behavior seeps into your soul, a subtle shaming that results in soul loss. Shame for being a woman who dares to sit in rooms with men, shame for having a brain and ambition and not just being "someone they fucked." Shame feels like a big goopy pile of sludge that grows bigger and bigger in your gut. For me, it eventually explodes into a huge cloud, and I disappear underneath it. Suffocating under a blanket of blackness, I go dark, silent, and frozen right there in the meeting or at the dinner table. Maybe a few hours or days later the blob subsides, but it's always ready to come back at a moment's notice. Like an unexpected puddle waiting on the sidewalk, almost invisible until you step in it.

What's a girl to do but focus on building her own powerful ego to withstand such an attack? To perfect her "work" mask, the protective shield she dons before heading into the office to fight these dragons? I put on a fancy look each day and wear it like a protective cloak. Not unlike the one I visualize in my work life today, when I head into a difficult intervention. But in my Hollywood days, I have no awareness of either having an internal light to protect, or that it is possible to protect it from vampires appearing in the form of old men who think they own Hollywood.

Following *Wedding Crashers* my mask has never been so strong, so much so that I'm starting to believe it myself. I'm at the center of something the industry calls "the wheel of comedy," a group of comedy actors, writers, and directors (triple threats) who together can create their own movie packages. I'm matching like-minded creatives with others of similar sensibilities. (A skill I still use today, only now I'm pulling together the right care team for each client I meet.) This flips the normal Hollywood cycle, where a studio buys a script and brings it to an actor or director. Instead, I'm putting movies together— complete with actors, writers, directors, and maybe produc- ers—and bringing them to the studio with everyone already committed. Comedy actors are versatile but also specific, and I love packaging a script that lets their souls shine through. My favorite moment is pitching one of my clients an idea and seeing their eyes light up. Bringing out the best in them. Whether my own soul is on fire doesn't matter as much to me as whether my clients are becoming who they're meant to be.

Vince and I, specifically, are emerging together. He's sud- denly commanding four times the salary he'd gotten before *Wedding Crashers*, and together we package his next movie, *The Break-Up*. But as both of our profiles are increasing, so is the tension between us. Where our calls used to have the feeling of mutual celebration, now they feel like a hungry void. Before, we were a team; now suddenly it's my job to bring more, big- ger, better. It used to be that we wanted to "get there," and we were doing it together. But once you achieve that kind of fame and recognition, it becomes an endless cycle. Suddenly "there" isn't enough anymore. Whereas before there was room to play and try things out and see if they worked, now failure and mis- takes are no longer an option. Everything needs to be perfect; the upward trajectory must not be interrupted.

The next opportunity comes along: this time, it's for the perfect Christmas movie. Vince will play the role of Santa Claus's brother, which just by itself sounds hilarious. But the stakes are so high now that the fun is gone. The paycheck is now double what Vince commanded for *The Break-Up*. I watch *Fred Claus* for the first time and feel a sinking feeling. It's good in a big, family-movie kind of way. But it lacks the edgy

Wedding Crasher vibe, which we were going for—or I *thought* we were going for, given this was meant to be an R-rated comedy. And it's not just me. There's something in the screening room that agents can sense a mile away: fear. This movie is not "a hit." At least, not yet. The race is on to try and fix it. From that place of fear, we're all gasping for control like the last breath of air. Chaos breaks out between the creatives.

It happens to be my birthday when all the creatives on the movie—plus the agents and the studio execs—get called into the Warner Brothers chairman's private office for lunch. Think of it as the school principal trying to calm the kids down. But that doesn't really work with movie stars. I look around this table of ten people and am very aware that it's me and nine men. They're all talking over one another. At one point, two of them almost reach over the table to smack each other. I sit quietly. Amid the ruckus I feel no desire to join the fight. I don't want to yell, be bitchy, or stage an attack. Instead, I witness the scene. And in the center of the storm, I hear a quiet voice speaking to me.

Is this really how you want to spend your birthday? it asks, gently. *In these rooms that you couldn't wait to get into?*

The answer is obvious: *No.* I wait for the meeting to end and get in my car with a new attitude. I am finally starting to see myself. It's the first stirring of my soul, coming back to life.

———

Do I MATTER? *How am I going to get out of this?*

It's the first thought that runs through my head that morning, when I wake up and remember it's my five-year sober birthday. I have been wearing my "Lisa Hallerman, talent agent" mask for so long, I barely know who I am beyond that. Accomplishing 365 days of consecutive sobriety, five years in a row, is a tall order. But I have arrived, and it feels unexpectedly empty. It's been two years since *Wedding Crashers* made box-office history, and I've hit all the career benchmarks I could have hoped for: I've made partner at the agency, I'm the head of the talent department, and I have a revolving seat on the board. But rather than feeling joy that I've "made it," I feel the golden handcuffs getting tighter by the day. I am tethered to some of the most famous movie stars in the world, and I feel like I'm disappearing. I've gotten everything I ever thought I wanted, but I am losing something far more important in the process.

I am living a life that is enormously privileged, with all the glitter and glamour a person could ask for. But this is the thing about the soul: it doesn't care. It's not interested in fame or money or sports cars or movie credits. While I had the kind of life many people dream about, it wasn't the life for me. My soul wanted something else. I appeared to be on top of the world, but in truth I was drowning. Lying in bed, I take stock. But it seems like I've traded addiction to drugs and alcohol for another obsession: self-importance and empty success. I'm trying to fill the void of soul loss with work. After eight years of fighting to "make it" in Hollywood, I've accomplished all I set out to do. So why do I feel so desperate? I'm at a crossroads and I know it. My soul is stirring, craving the most important thing: meaning. I don't just need a life *upgrade*. I need a complete life *pivot*. But I have no idea what my options are yet. So I decide to buckle down, accept my lot, and keep doing what

I'm doing. Soul, however, has other plans. Finding me an un-willing listener, its messages keep getting louder.

One evening I am in my car driving home from work when my phone rings. It's a number I don't recognize, but in my business you always answer the phone.

"Lisa, I'm sorry to bother you," says the voice at the other end of the line. "This is Erica's mom." She sounds frail, dis-turbed. Erica is twenty-five years old and one of my up-and-coming, new-and-exciting clients. *Why is her mother calling me?*

"Oh, well . . . hi?" I say, a bit confused.

"There has been an incident," she says. "Erica's on her way to the hospital in an ambulance."

Looking back, I don't remember much from the conver-sation. I don't remember asking *which hospital*, though I must have. I don't remember hanging up the phone, though I must have done that too. The only thing I remember other than the word "ambulance" is another phrase. A trigger phrase.

Suicide attempt.

I pull over to the side of the road as my body starts to tremble. The tears are running down my face and a familiar feeling overtakes me. I open the car door quickly and all at once I am crying and sick and throwing up on the side of the road. It takes a few minutes, and I'm not sure how I manage it, but I clean myself up enough to drive home.

I sit in my driveway waiting for the knot in my stomach to resolve, but it doesn't. Soon I get the next call: She is go-ing to be okay. She already wants to talk about going back to work and what that looks like, so she is asking if I can come by and see her. But I'm not okay. Erica tried to do what Andy succeeded at, all those years earlier. The circumstances are totally different, but suddenly I'm revisiting a deep wound I have never really looked at. A wound that hasn't healed, as I'd imagined it would have after this many years in sobriety. I have not yet done my trauma work, which means the wound has been simply lying in wait—ready to rise up the minute a similar circumstance crosses my path.

The next morning I drive to the hospital on my way to work. I find myself planning to say to Erica what I'd always wished I'd had a chance to say to Andy. If he'd been granted a "day after the attempt"—a chance to try life again.

I go to Erica's bedside. She's half-awake, and I just start talking. I'm diving into my thoughts with no filter. I ramble about mental health, addiction, twelve-step programs, shame, and God. I'm coming unraveled, vomiting every thought I'd ever wanted to say to Andy. In the midst of the rant, I look up and see Erica. She does not look impressed. I realize I've misstepped and try to back out of my tirade. I close by reminding her of the devastation one can leave in their wake and tell her I'm there to help. But something changes between me and Erica in the hospital room that day. The speech I've given is for me, not her. It's my attempt to soothe my own trigger; it isn't really about Erica. Such self-focus is not what an actor thinks they need from their agent. It's the beginning of the end of my working relationship with Erica. She decides to leave the agency soon afterward.

I leave the hospital feeling deeply disturbed. I am aware of a pain inside of me that I haven't felt in a very long time. I don't know it at the time, but the process of reigniting my soul has begun. Cracks are forming in the foundation of who

I've thought myself to be. The ground beneath me is breaking, so my roots can finally grow back down into the deep and
important places they'd withdrawn from out of trauma. The
price of this growth? I'm about to confront my deepest fears.

As I walk into the office that morning, I don't feel like
Lisa Hallerman, head of the talent department. I'm not sure *who*
I am anymore. I feel vulnerable, malleable, and unfamiliar to
myself as I walk into the conference room for my meeting
with Reed. Reed was hired by UTA to do a 360-degree review
of the board of directors and the partners. This meant he interviewed everyone who worked for and with me, as well as
those I worked for. The other board members, partners, all the
agents. Recording their answers anonymously, he grilled them
about me. This was their opportunity to provide feedback they
might not have felt comfortable giving me directly. Today is
the moment of truth. In front of him on the table is a black
notebook filled with what my colleagues *really* think of me.

I apologize to Reed for being out of it, explaining that I've
just come from the hospital.

"We don't have to do this today," he says kindly.

"No," I reply. "Today is perfect. I'm broken open and I'm
ready to hear whatever you've got." I can feel that change
is upon me as he opens the big black binder. I see that Reed
has color-coded all the negative statements in red ink. From
across the table I see a *lot* of red. As we start reading through
the comments together, a common theme emerges. *Ego.* The
person I want to be, the person I know I am, deep down, is
not the person anyone sees. They see a mask, an ego-mask
of a successful agent who has become the classic Hollywood

agent. The one who yells so her voice can be heard down the hall. Who makes condescending remarks. Who sides with the winning team and rarely stops to help the underdog. Who believes that emotion is a sign of weakness, and who leaves those who are most vulnerable—those who need her leadership—feeling alone. In other words, I've become one of *them*. I've carefully learned the role of "Hollywood agent" from what I've seen around me, and I am executing it to perfection.

In some cases the feedback is coming from those who see in me what they most hate in themselves. We are all in the same boat, so to speak. But what is clear to me, sitting at that conference table, is that my outsides do not match my insides—and that I am willing to do whatever it takes to align the two.

I hand my "agent" mask to Reed that day as I hug him good-bye. I've never forgotten him, and I keep that binder to this day as a reminder. It's the best gift UTA ever gave me.

OVER THE NEXT few weeks I feel myself withdrawing, keeping quiet in meetings—and feeling stuck. I look at the black binder and I know what it's telling me to do. I need to change my life completely, but I don't have the courage. But just as I feel the golden handcuffs tightening again, life does for me what I cannot do for myself.

Suddenly and without warning, Vince is no longer taking my calls. Vince, the goofy comedian I'd met years earlier and had determined to make a star. Who I've nurtured and championed all the way to $20 million per film. Whom I've spoken to no fewer than fifteen times per day, often for hours at a time, for years. Suddenly not talking to me. It's not uncommon for a client to get annoyed at their agent, or to go quiet for a period of time while they go into their craft a bit. But it's been three months. Every day the feelings get a little louder. I'm feeling scared, sad, and—worst of all—powerless. It's not like he's halfway around the world on set; he's shooting a movie right here in LA and he won't take my calls. I lose sleep.

I'm convinced Vince is firing me. That he's been wooed by another agent, someone promising him bigger things, better things. *Ego-supporting things.* Bordering on despair, I go to the board at UTA and ask for advice. They come back with the consensus that I should drive across town and see Vince on set. I ask for backup, someone to come with me—but no one volunteers. *Okay,* I think cautiously. *Maybe this will work?* I mean, if I can see him in person, he has to remember who I am. Who *we* are. Vince has been my co-conspirator, my creative partner, and my friend for almost a decade. Together we've come up with countless ideas for movies, plotted his future, charted our dreams. I've worked better and more creatively with him than anyone else in my career. But now I'm learning the hard way that there is a difference between a *client* and a *friend.* Vince is showing himself to be the former, not the latter.

I pull into the driveway at the film studio and park my car among the cast trailers sitting off to the side. A production assistant comes up to the car.

"Who are you here to see?" he asks.

"Hi, I'm Lisa," I say. "Vince's agent."

"Oh, hi, Lisa," he says. "What's up?"

"Um, I'm here to see Vince?" It's as if I'm asking this young PA for permission. He walks away from the car and speaks into his walkie-talkie. Soon he turns back toward me.

"He's on set right now and doesn't want any visitors," the PA reports. This is something I've never heard before. In the past, Vince was *dying* to have me come to set.

"I just want to speak to him when he has a break," I say, trying to seem normal. "He must have lunch coming up. I'll just wait until he comes back to his trailer." The PA looks at me.

"Okay," he says warily. "But you will have to wait in your car here. I can't let you on set." He walks away. I'm not quite sure what emotion I am feeling just yet. A bit numb for sure. But also willfully hopeful, like this will all get cleared up in a moment. As soon as the PA is out of earshot I call Vince's assistant.

"Hey, it's me," I say. "I want to speak to Vince in person during lunch. Please tell this PA that I can park my car."

"Lisa," the assistant responds, sounding almost scared. "He doesn't want to see you. He's asking that you go home."

I take a deep breath. I think I might cry, but instead I start laughing. The truth is out—Vince doesn't want to see me. Game over. The fear and sadness I've been feeling vaporizes, and the powerlessness I've been feeling goes with it. In its place I feel the hot burning fire of anger. To avoid exploding in homicidal rage on set—which would be unacceptable sober behavior—I pull out of the parking lot and head back to the office.

Back at UTA, I walk straight into the office of one of the board members and explain what just happened. How I tried to see Vince, but he didn't want to see me. So I left. "That's not what Richard Lovett would have done," he tells me. Richard is the chairman of CAA. "Well, first of all, I am not trying to be Richard Lovett," I snap. "Second of all, if *you* want to be Richard, then you could have come with me. Third, go fuck yourself." Okay, so that last part I keep to myself.

In the light of the truth about Vince, another emerges from deep within me. *I no longer want this.* "This" being everything I previously thought I needed to be happy. So-called success and glitz and glory. This job is no longer feeding my soul; in fact, it's sucking the life out of me. I need a life full of meaning and purpose and passion, and I'm not getting it here.

A couple of weeks later, after filming wraps, he finally calls. My assistant practically screams, *Vince on line one!* I take a deep breath and pick up the phone.

"Hello," I say.

"Hey, girlie," he replies, patronizingly. "So, this is the hardest phone call I have ever had to make." That's quite enough for me—I don't need to hear any more. After all, I've been listening to him yammer on for a decade. Now it's my turn. All the unresolved trauma of a lifetime comes bubbling to the surface in an unrelenting rage. I stand up and turn my back to the door of the office, as if that will muffle the sounds of what's about to come out of my mouth. Glaring out at Beverly Hills, I begin to scream everything I've wanted to say for years but have never dared. Looking back I see that my diatribe was not all about him—it was a career's worth of resentment at Hollywood. At the mean-spiritedness, the shaming, the finger-pointing. Years of pent-up anger from fighting a battle I could never win. Of having to prove that I, as a woman, was worthy and good enough to represent a movie star like him. Of trying to be better than the best, to make up for the fact that I didn't fit the mold of the guy in the expensive suit playing eighteen holes with his clients at the Riviera, or throwing parties at their mansions, or driving matching Maseratis. I am done competing. I am done having my self-worth be contingent on another person—a movie star, a boss, or anyone else.

So there I am, yelling like a madwoman, months and years of pent-up anger rushing out in a wildfire. I'm talking so much I'm not allowing the best gabber on the planet to get a word in. But eventually I have to catch my breath, and he takes his opportunity.

"This has all been very tough for me," he says. "I've tried to act like it hasn't been. I don't think I have anything left to give." I pause. Those lines . . . those lines are familiar to me.

"Are you quoting me lines from *The Break-Up*?" I demand, incredulous. I've seen the movie no less than fifty times, what with all the screenings and note sessions that take place before a movie comes out. Both of us know every line by heart.

"Yes," he admits. "I think it's relevant."

My life has become a dramatic comedy, I think. I hang up, and the truth comes rushing in: *I have to get out. I need to flee. I need to escape.*

In a few years I'll recognize that Vince firing me is the best thing that has ever happened to me. Eventually I'll even make amends to him for my behavior on the phone that day and we talk about the growth each one of us has gone through over the years. But I don't know any of that now. Right now, all I know is survival. When pushed to our limits, we revert to old habits in a split second—following the first impulse that arises. Like any good addict—even in recovery—I look for the nearest exit. I pick up the phone and within twenty-four hours I'm working across the street at a rival agency, Endeavor.

CHAPTER EIGHT

Reconnecting to Soul

I'm just walking out of Pilates, feeling really good. Ready to face a day of RMA client meetings and phone calls. I turn on my phone and see a text from Sara, the mother of a young addict I worked with six years ago. We'd done months of family therapy and trauma work, in hopes her son could successfully get sober from heroin.

Elisa, the text reads. *Lennox overdosed last night. He's gone, Elisa. I really need some help.*

I'm frozen there on the sidewalk, not yet in my car. I close my eyes and take a few deep breaths. I get to the car and when I'm seated begin to cry. This is a deep cry, from the depths of my soul. I'm crying for Lennox, who I know wanted to be sober but struggled repeatedly with his unresolved trauma and harrowing addiction. I'm crying for his family, for his friends, and for all the other souls I know who've lost their lives to addiction. I am also crying for myself, keenly aware as I am that I dodged death more times than were my fair share. I'm crying because I got lucky and because I'm grateful to be sober. And I'm crying to be so vividly reminded to respect the disease, which is always with me, regardless of my abstinence. For each person who dies of this disease, hundreds of others get a wake-up call just like this and many lives are saved.

Now that I have stopped crying and checked in with a sober friend to talk about my own grief, I pick up the phone to call Sara. She answers.

"Oh, Elisa," she says, crying. "He just couldn't do it anymore. I pray he has the peace he had been searching for all this time."

"I hope so too, Sara," I respond. And even as she grieves, I explain that when one addict dies, countless other lives are saved. Every time a sober addict hears of someone dying of the disease of addiction, we know that could have been us. We were spared this time, but it reminds us how fragile our sobriety is and strengthens our resolve.

"I have been scared about this day for as long as I can remember," she says through her tears. "I thought I would be prepared, since he's been living on the street for so long. But now that it's here, I feel like I'm dying too. Last night I was lying on the floor, screaming in a pain I could never have imagined. You taught us all about trauma, and this is the greatest trauma of my life. I'm afraid it's going to kill me." She's sobbing.

I can hear Sara's bravery and wisdom shining through.

I tell her, "You are a true hero, a mother who is doing for herself what, unfortunately, you could never have done for Lennox. Despite how much you loved him, and how much you tried."

We hang up and I am reminded of the power of doing our own healing work. When we let it guide us, soul will show us the way out of even the darkest days. I know Sara's excruciating pain will never be gone, but I also know that once she begins to heal, it will transform into deep purpose. I make some calls and work on setting up grief counselors, trauma experts, and treatment to follow—for Sara and the entire family.

—

WHAT HAPPENS WHEN we are ready to heal our trauma is that we increasingly get pointed back in the direction of our own soul—and it's usually a pretty rough ride. The day Vince fires me, I crash into a need I've been ignoring for a long time: the need for a major life change. Unfortunately, the biggest change I can muster is to quit UTA and cross Wilshire Boulevard to Endeavor. I'm still in the same job, having the same kind of days. Yes, it's a course adjustment that makes a big difference to my internal state, but it's not as if I've left my feelings of anger and resentments behind. I'm still *me*. My soul is in desperate need of more drastic change, but my mind is not ready. I still believe my happiness and fulfillment are tied to what's happening outside of me—in this case, the company I'm working for and the clients on my list. I walk into the Endeavor building on my first day of work feeling confident, but within a few weeks my confidence is waning. My partner from UTA ended up leaving for Endeavor at the same time, and her clients begin to follow her over. It's obvious to everyone that mine do not. I succumb to self-doubt, sure I must not be any good at this job anymore. I must have lost my ability to agent well, be creative, or be a skillful negotiator. The trauma Post-it Notes from Vince's departure start to pile up in my psyche, planting insecurity where previously there was none. I'm starting to wonder if I'm ever going to feel good enough again.

Moreover, I'm not yet *aware* my soul is driving this change. My partners at the agency are supportive, passing me in the hall saying things like, "Chin up, you'll get them back." There's a new whisper coming from within, something very quiet that's asking me, *Do you even want them back?* But it's soft enough I cannot yet hear it.

For the next few months I sit in staff meetings and have nothing to say. These meetings are where we agents discuss the projects our clients are working on and brainstorm new projects moving forward. I have no clients to speak of, no big projects on the horizon. It puts me in an unfamiliar place of feeling vulnerable and paralyzed. But two things are clear. First, I am *aware* that I am paralyzed. This is new. I've somehow developed a witness inside my head who is capable of seeing what I'm doing, feeling, and saying from the position of an observer. I find myself daydreaming—in a creative way. I'm contemplating things I never had time to think about before, like, if I could have a new lifestyle, what would it look like? Second, my newfound observer observes that, without all the constant talking I am used to doing, I'm finally able to *listen*. I used to prepare carefully for staff meetings, and I loved sharing all my exciting news. Now I have nothing to share, but I find myself looking forward to these meetings anyway. I let my thoughts wander and end up thinking about the achievements I've had in Hollywood, how proud I am of what I've accomplished. I start to see more clearly what was under my control, and what was not. *God, grant me the serenity to accept the things I cannot change, the courage to change the things I can, and the wisdom to know the difference.* Slowly, my soul's truth dawns: as fascinating and wonderful as the entertainment business will always be, I don't want to be a part of it anymore. The feeling is subtle at first. Then, after a few months, it starts burning inside of me. For the first time in my life, I am curious about the pain and discomfort I'm feeling. Rather than pointing fingers at others, I am going deep; I am growing down, into myself. As a result of this dark night, I'm uncovering and discovering more about myself than I have in years.

The term "dark night" was first used by the great Spanish mystic and poet Saint John of the Cross (1542–1591), but it was the modern depth psychologist Thomas Moore who coined the term "dark night of the soul." In his book of the same title, he proposes that the purpose of pain is not to destroy you, but rather to aid in the care of your soul. Turning back toward my soul is the true gift of the dark night that started on that phone call with Vince. The rupture is too huge to ignore, so I am forced to acknowledge that something is not working. I have to excavate the defects of my own character that had brought me to this place. In the process I am able to start reconnecting the essence of my soul and reestablishing my connection to source.

I start putting together lists of things I've always wanted for myself. *Spend more time on the East Coast near my family. Be of service to the addiction community. Take some classes and learn something new. Travel for fun. Work from anywhere.* I begin to lay plans for my future, finally seeing that I am the architect of my own life. I really don't want to dress the part of "high-powered Hollywood agent" anymore. I want a job where I don't have to wear fancy shoes; I want to wear flip flops or, better yet, go barefoot. I want a job where I get to be outside, sitting in the sun during the day—instead of just watching it through the conference room windows. I want to be able to leave LA for a month if I want to and work from new and interesting places, meeting new people. Learning new things. I reconnect with my childhood desire to be a doctor. An ER doctor, to be specific. I have no idea if this is even possible, given I am in my midforties, and I can't imagine diving into medical school. *But hey*, I think, *no need to rule anything out.* I start to do research on prerequisite classes at UCLA when I stumble onto a course in drug and alcohol counseling. The more I read, the more excited I get. I feel inspired in a way I haven't in a very long time. I begin to realize that you can truly find new sources of inspiration if you just go looking. Even something as small as taking a class becomes a clue that will lead me to many things to come. I decide to start taking night classes a couple nights a week. Suddenly I'm reignited with purpose. The agent meetings where I once felt paralyzed and vulnerable turn into productive study time, as I survey my notecards from behind a folder. My whole life lights up now that I am studying something I am truly interested in. I love how it makes me feel. I'm feeding my soul.

In addition, I'm making new friends and am starting to hear a new word—one that speaks to me on a deep level: *trauma*. I've been sober for nine years, but I've never thought about my past trauma nor done any healing work. It's still a pile of muck just hanging out in my body, clouding my soul from view. The more I read about trauma, the more I see that what I've taken for post-sobriety "healing" is just another set of masks and invisible parts. Better, more well-adapted parts, yes. But still coping mechanisms to keep my unresolved trauma at bay.

A few years earlier, I had met the spiritual teacher Gabby Bernstein. Around the time she released her first book, *Add More ~ing To Your Life,* a mutual friend had invited me to one of her retreats in Costa Rica. I hadn't heard of Gabby before, and after looking into her I thought, *I'm either going to love her or hate her.* From the moment we met, she became one of my dearest friends—as well as an important teacher in my life in so many ways.

Around the time I'm starting to take classes at UCLA, Gabby calls to ask if I can take the next weekend off. She wants me to come to the East Coast for a workshop with her healer. Just the word "healer" sends my eyes rolling, but she manages to convince me. There are a lot of people at the event, everyone dressed in white. The healer puts us through a very complicated ceremony. We meditate, pray, and then they ask what type of healing each of us wants to receive. I know exactly what to ask for: *I want to know what to do next.* As each of us receives an individualized energetic healing, I'm eagerly awaiting a download of direction and meaning. I expect something big to happen, but I experience nothing.

At the end of the weekend, Gabby is glowing. The whole way home she can't stop talking about how amazing her healing was, how she feels cracked wide open and is vibrating at a higher frequency than before the weekend, blah blah blah.

"Um, Gabs?" I say. "I don't think it worked for me."

"Wait," she says. "Give it time."

Annoying, I think. *Why did she get the power healing, and not me?*

As soon as I get back to LA, the opportunity I've been waiting for arrives: one of my successful former clients from UTA agrees to meet with me. He's twenty minutes late to the restaurant, giving me ample time to plan my speech in my head. How I'm thriving, how Endeavor is an uplevel in so many ways. I'm planning my *Jerry Maguire* moment, cataloguing the incompetencies and flaws of the UTA agents he's working with now, building a narrative that proves my worth by contrast. Finally, I'm going to map out the plan I've devised for his continued success if he comes over to Endeavor.

Eventually he arrives, and I launch into my planned speech. But something is wrong. Whereas I used to be able to write a speech in my head and execute it flawlessly, I cannot do it. The fact is, I don't *want* to convince him of my worth. I don't *want* to talk trash about my former colleagues. Not five minutes after he sits down, I drop the Jerry Maguire mask, knowing that doing so means I have no chance of winning this client back. But the cracks in my armor have gotten too big, and my soul is no longer quietly sitting in the backseat. She's taken the wheel.

I make an appointment to speak to Ari, my boss at Endeavor. As soon as I'm in his office, I present my case.

"I need to move to New York," I tell him. "I still want to be an agent, but I want to work out of the NYC office. That way I can be closer to my family." In truth, getting to be closer to my family is an added bonus; the real reason I want to move is because, for whatever reason, I believe getting out of LA will reignite my interest in the job and solve all my problems.

Either believing that New York would be good for me—or trying to get rid of me, I'll never know—he agrees to the transfer. Within a few weeks I'm in New York looking at apartments and meeting with one of the board members of Endeavor's NYC office, Jennifer Walsh. I've never met Jen before, but I've long been very impressed by her career success. Truth be told, I'm a little nervous to meet her. But I'm so excited for my new venture that I figure we'll be fast friends, working closely together and taking NY by storm.

The day before the meeting with Jen, I'm touring apartments with my dad. He's made yet another life transformation and is now killing it as a top real estate broker in NYC. Our relationship has come a long way in the last decade since I got sober, and we are as close now as we've ever been. He proudly shows me dreamy apartments in Soho and Tribeca, any one of which should have made me happy. But somehow nothing seems right. The last place we look at checks all the boxes on the long list of "needs" I had given him, but I stand in the middle of the living room with tears streaming down my face. He looks at me and realizes they aren't happy tears.

"What's the matter?" he asks.

"I don't know," I sob. "This doesn't feel right."

He sees I'm struggling. "What is it, honey?"

"I don't think I should live in New York. It's not me. I live in LA."

He takes me to lunch at the deli down the block, and I am still crying. Over sandwiches he asks me if I remember what he told me when I called and told him I didn't want to be a lawyer anymore. I nod yes, smiling.

"Well," he says. "I still think the same thing. Just do what makes you happy. Whatever it is, do it and the rest will work out." I start to relax.

"I love you," he continues. "And you will figure it out, I'm sure of it."

"Thank you, Dad," I say, wiping my tears. "I love you, too."

He is right: I'm definitely not happy. What I don't know yet is what to *do* about that.

The next day I walk into Jen's office, hoping she'll help me turn this ship around. I imagine her showing me a brand-new office with a great view and promising to mentor me through the awkward "new job" period. I have my fingers crossed that I'll walk out of our meeting suddenly thrilled about the New York move.

Her office is very big and very . . . fluffy. It's filled with the kind of couches where you get lost in cushions and need a hand to get up when the meeting is over. She is sitting in a winged chair across from me looking very regal while I'm feeling like a child sunk deep into the couch.

"How are you doing?" she asks me.

"I'm great!" I lie. I can sense she knows the truth.

"So, you're ready to move across the country and start a new life in New York?" she asks.

"Well, I mean, it's not a *new* life," I say, getting nervous. "I grew up here. But I think so? I mean *yes*. Yes, I do want to start something new." I glance up to see a look of skepticism on Jen's face.

"Lisa, maybe you're done with this part of your life," she says matter-of-factly. "Others are starting to talk and want to take your title away if you don't start agenting the way you once did." The truth of it hits me. She's right: this is not what I want anymore. But leaving the golden handcuffs and facing the blank canvas of life after Hollywood is terrifying.

I sit frozen, holding back tears, too afraid to utter a word lest I lose it right there in her office. So I have no choice but to listen. The more she says, the more I can feel the blood drain out of my face, and the more I want to disappear into the shabby-chic upholstery. I walked into this office expecting Jen to be my future partner in crime, and here she is pulling away the rest of the mask I have been too afraid to tear off myself. She's not only looking at me, she is *seeing* me. All of me. I feel exposed, as if she just pierced a hole all the way through me, exposing my deepest vulnerabilities. I am not ready to have this deeper level of conversation. So I shut down my feelings, block the tide of pure fear that threatens to drown me and extract myself from that venus flytrap of a couch, and make a beeline out of her office and the building. As I stand on the corner, the pretzel man kindly hands me napkins to blow my nose. I call the only person in the city I know who I think can help me through this colossal breakdown: Gabby.

"You were right about the healing taking time," I say when I get her on the phone. "I feel it now, I'm totally cracked open. But it's still not working how it's supposed to, because I don't feel blissful. I'm having a nervous breakdown! My whole life is crashing and I am in pieces."

"Congratulations!" she says. "Come over to my apartment *now*."

I sit at her dining room table and begin to calm down.

"You have to crack open for the light to get in," she explains. "You are finally allowing yourself to heal on a deep level. Your whole life is reordering itself, and everything will be as it should be moving forward." I let it sink in, because it feels true. That feeling is all I have, but somehow it is enough.

Back in LA, I go see my boss, Ari.

"I can't move to NY," I say as soon as I walk in the door.

"Why?" he asks. I decide not to tell him about the conversation I had with Jen, though part of me wants to.

"I just don't feel it's the right decision for me right now," I say. "I am having an existential crisis and I thought NY would fix it, but it won't. I'm not sure what I want to do with my life. But it's not moving to NYC. Can you give me just a few months to figure things out?" Ari looks at me and I'm sure I'm about to get fired. Who tells their boss they don't know if they want their job and then asks for time to do the inner work to decide?

"Okay," he finally says. "But you better figure it out fast."

I thank him and leave the office. In the hallway, I take a deep breath and relief floods through me. He didn't have any obligation to let me keep my job, but like the gracious soul he is, he did.

Meanwhile, I am talking such trash about Jen in my head, I can't even begin to tell you. Cursing her every day. *How dare she?! She doesn't know me! Who does she think she is? Fuck her!* But on another level, I know she is right. Even through my resentment, I feel she's named what I already know in my soul: I have begun to transform. I am no longer Lisa Hallerman, top talent agent. I'm just Elisa, a regular person with human foibles and flaws, trying to figure out what she wants to do with her life.

Years later I will be able to thank Jen for having such an honest conversation with me—a conversation I needed more than anything. She illuminated a narrative I was telling myself and reminded me there was another way. Years later after leaving the business and starting my new career, I returned to the office—this time choosing the chair—and thanked her for her honesty and insight. She went on to be one of my biggest supporters in beginning to write.

This kind of alchemical transformation happens for all of us at different times, right at the moment we're ready for it. The raw material of our wounds and our masks and our trauma gets worked and reworked until it turns into gold—in this case, wisdom. This process of "getting worked" is not just essential to the healing process, it *is* the process. The painful events in our lives are our teachers. The father of depth psychology, Carl Jung, was perhaps the first to use the metaphor of alchemy as a way of describing self-healing, comparing each of the alchemical stages to the process of personal awakening. First the substance of our lives has to heat up, in the "fire" stage. Then comes the "killing" stage, where burned ashes symbolize death or a dark night of the soul. The healing begins in the "water" stage, dissolving old habits and purifying past wounds. Then the "earth" phase arrives where everything comes back together, integrating the experience. Finally, in the "air" phase, your being is elevated into something completely new.

There is no reconnecting to our essence without living through dark nights, sitting with them, and allowing them to fully transform us into something beautiful. While waiting for that transformation, we must be patient. But that doesn't mean stagnant: we can use this time to nurture and feel and get to know our soul. Find what we love and do more of it. Find people we love and spend more time with them. Find places that make us feel safe and spend more time in them.

I start to reframe my situation. I realize that, exactly like my addiction, the unhappiness I feel in my current job isn't a problem to be fixed. Rather, it's the dawning of new awareness. I am suddenly clear that this career is no longer fulfilling, and my being is craving something different. I have changed and grown, and with that transformation I need more depth and a new purpose. Leaving the entertainment business is not a failure, as I once would have believed. It's about closing a successful and important chapter in my journey, and moving on to my next achievement. I'm redefining what the word "success" means to me, distinguishing between material success and the success that comes from being in my purpose. I'm finding my way back to being proud of myself for all that I've done over the past twelve years, while acknowledging that I have much more to give and am ready to move on to something new.

Meantime, I am devouring my classes at UCLA. I read a book or article that moves me, and like the agent I am, I immediately pick up the phone and call the author. Often I go see them in person. I am using the skill set I've built as an agent to build a network of experts in various areas including trauma-focused recovery, neuroscience, and addiction psychiatry. I'm ravenous to learn more. I read the books that were cited in the books that are required reading. I find I'm especially interested in learning about the treatment center aspect of recovery, so I volunteer at Friendly House, an all-female sober living home for women. A sober living home is what's called a "step down" solution, meaning it's a place people go when they leave a residential treatment facility. There is no clinical or medical treatment provided, it's just a sober place to live for a period of time, supported by staff. It provides a community for clients, giving them a safe place to begin to integrate back into life while maintaining some of the structure that was helpful in treatment. At Friendly House I run a group for six to eight women, once or twice a week during my lunch break. I am surprised how much value I find in my time there. I feel purposeful, sharing some of my own new insights with the girls. I also listen hard to their stories, learning a lot about what is and is not working for them during their recovery.

During this same period my sober friend Zoe recommends a book called *The Soul's Code: In Search of Character and Calling* by James Hillman. Hillman is a psychologist who founded the archetypal psychology movement. In the book he explains his "acorn theory": just as an acorn already possesses the design to become an oak tree inside, each human also has an innate plan that is eager to be realized and created. This theory suggests to me that my life plan is already formed inside of me; all I need to do is actualize the image that already exists. Somehow this makes perfect sense to me. Part of what's allowing me to make these huge pivots in my life is the belief that I intuitively know exactly what to do. I keep referring back to the list I made of what interested me when I was a little girl, what I saw myself doing "when I grew up." Rather than seeing these dreams as childhood fairy tales, suddenly I see them as the blueprint in my acorn.

I notice as I read that the term "soul" keeps leaping out at me throughout the book. Soul, as Hillman talks about it, feels distinctly different from the concepts I've known before, like my higher power or the universe at large. Soul is unique to *me*. It's the plan that's inside of me, that has been guiding my life path since I was born. We can listen to soul with more or less attention, but it's there even if we ignore it. I begin to understand the big turning points that have happened to me recently as soul-driven and purposeful. I'm relieved when I realize that the plans for my private oak tree don't need to be worked on or created outside of me. The information I'd asked for during my weekend with Gabby and the healer—to know what I was supposed to do next—has been inside of me all along.

≡

My UCLA classes and my time at Friendly House now complete, I come up with an idea: I'll open a sober living home for young men. I choose to open a male sober living home for two reasons: first, after working with almost all male clients as an agent, I feel confident I can handle male personalities. Unlike the obstacles I'm constantly used to hitting in my Hollywood career, pretty much as soon as I start talking out loud about this idea, things start to flow. My dear friend Fiona already runs a sober house for women, and she's willing to jump in and teach me everything I need to begin. Within a week of telling her about my new idea, she calls to let me know that she and her partner have been looking at a house to rent—but they'd decided not to take it. She thinks I should grab the house, which is in the perfect location, and use it to start my sober living home.

I rent the house, decorate it, put a plan together, and hire staff. Within a matter of weeks I am ready to open it. I start slowly, with two guys in the house and a live-in employee. I

168

am nervous; I have families trusting me with their children. I begin to wonder if I know enough to be doing this. While a clinical background is not required to own and operate a sober living home—like most addiction treatment, these homes are not regulated—I realize it's going to need more of me than I am able to give while working at Endeavor. I'm going to have to quit my job.

But the question of *when* keeps me up nights. I even find myself pestering personal growth and spirituality author Marianne Williamson to give me my cue to leave. I'd met her a few years back, introduced by Gabby. Back then Marianne was looking for some help getting a project started in the entertainment industry, and when Gabby asked me to join them for lunch I was as excited as if she'd asked me to dine with her and Brad Pitt.

Now I am sitting in my office at Endeavor, on the phone with Marianne. Our relationship is theoretically about me helping *her*, but somehow I'm the one who always gets the benefit from our calls. She's like a wise sage who has shown up to guide me into the next phase of my soul's journey.

"When am I going to be done with this job?" I ask her. I have another year left on my contract with Endeavor, but it's already a lot of work running the sober house at the same time. I don't think I could add school to the mix without something breaking.

"You will know when you know," she says.

Typical Marianne answer, I think.

"Obviously," I say. "But I am asking *you* when you think I will know!"

"That is your ego, Lisa, wanting to know the future," she says. "The future hasn't happened yet. So there is nothing to know for sure."

Oy vey, I think. I am still getting used to these types of open answers. Today I have a similar line I offer when clients ask me when they'll be done with treatment.

"Can you hold on for a minute?" I ask, and they always say yes. "Great, I just need to grab my crystal ball." There's a pause and, in rare instances, a laugh. But then I give the real explanation.

"There are two phases of knowing something's time," I say. "The first phase is when you say to yourself, *I think I'm ready to leave treatment.* Or, *I think I'm ready to move.* Or, *I think I'm ready to break up.* Or, *I think I'm going to retire.* This means it's not yet time.

"The second phase is when you know *from your heart* that this program, relationship, job, or home is no longer yours. That is a genuine and visceral knowing, and there is no question about it."

On August 23, 2011—my forty-third birthday—I finally have that visceral knowing. I walk into my office that morning and feel complete. My life and heart are now in Santa Monica, running this home. While I know the house is just the beginning of the new chapter, I am sure in my soul that the Hollywood chapter is over. I don't have an ounce of doubt. With no hesitation, no nervousness, and no appointment, I walk into my bosses' offices and let them know I'm retiring from agenting and starting a different life. I will be forever grateful for the kindness, support, and respect they showed me that day and in the years that followed.

As I leave, I almost can't believe I have the courage to do this. The challenge ahead is enormous. I am leaving the safety of a job that I have known for almost two decades, as well as a salary, health insurance, close colleagues, and the creature comforts of routine. But I know that if I do not jump off the metaphorical cliff, I will continue to wither away and die inside. I have no choice but to leap, knowing in my heart that life will never be the same again.

CHAPTER NINE

Returning Home

I am meeting with my clients, the Martin family, to prepare them for our intervention with their son and brother, William. We agree to meet at the parents' house to go over the letters one last time and remind the family why we are doing this and what we hope to accomplish today.

"The point of today is just to get William to agree to go from his house to treatment," I remind them. "Everything else that you want to say can be worked through in family therapy once he is safe and sound in rehab." William's mom nods as she begins to cry.

"I'm sorry," she apologizes. "I don't mean to cry. I hope I don't start to cry at William's house in the middle of my letter."

"Please do," I reassure her. "Crying is appropriate and human. If you need to stop and compose yourself, that's fine." I turn toward the rest of the family.

"What you are about to do is hard, but I will be with you the whole time," I say. "I will guide you every step. But I also want you to speak from your heart and soul. That's a very vulnerable thing to do, so it can feel scary. But it's important for you to access the deepest parts of yourselves, in order for William to drop the mask of addiction and feel into *his* heart and soul as well."

I compliment them on the latest drafts of their intervention letters and begin to pass them out at the table. They have worked really hard on these letters. For the first draft I instruct the family to follow my outline, which breaks the letter into three sections. In the first section they talk about the addict in their lives, laying out what they love, admire, or respect about them. I tell them to be as detailed as possible. This is not meant to be a laundry list of attributes, but really a time to give examples and tell stories really highlighting their strengths, personality, and warmth. I usually ask for three or four stories so we can then decide which ones are the strongest and make sure they are different from other family members'. The second section is where we begin with what I call "the howevers." *However, due to your alcohol or drug use I feel* . . . Here we also want to tell very specific stories of their behavior and how it has impacted them as a family member. It is important to use only "I feel" statements, so I have them go back and circle every time they write the word "you"—replacing it with an *I feel* or *I felt* statement. I include a long list of feeling words when I send the outline, so they can really tap into more precise and specific emotions. It is important in this section to tell the story of the addicted loved one's behavior through your own eyes. The loved one doesn't remember the incident in its totality, and certainly doesn't remember it from your point of view. This is an attempt to really connect from your heart to their heart. I explain to the family that it is important to hold their anger and resentment aside when writing the letters. While completely valid, that will be worked on later in family therapy. It is important to know there is always a vulnerable part of the addict that is exhausted and desperate for help, but that—in an intervention—you are often met partially by the voice of the addict or their disease. This part is usually covering up a fear that treatment won't work or a belief that they aren't worthy of such support.

The third and final section is "the ask" and the setting of boundaries. This is where they will ask their loved one directly to go to the treatment facility we've picked out for them. It is important to be clear what you are asking of your loved one, but not to be so specific as to be limiting. It also is a time to set boundaries and expectations, such as what kind of financial support you will continue to offer, how long you are willing to give them an opportunity to find alternative living situations, whether you are willing to continue the marriage or relationship, and whether they are allowed to see their children. It also includes what the consequences will be if they are unwilling to go to treatment today.

"You all did so well. I can tell you put a lot of hard work into these letters," I say. "I think they will really touch William in a way he needs right now." I go on to explain how everything will go. "When we walk in, we will ask William to join us in the living room. We'll all sit down. Mom, I would like you and Grace to sit next to him on the couch, one on either side. Dad, sit closest to the exit, in case he wants to leave. If he does, you can gently get up and guide him back to the couch. Same with Alex and Simon: sit in the chairs on either side of me and prepare to guide him back to his seat if he gets up.

"After we're seated, I will introduce myself. I'll let him know that we are here because you all love him so much. I will ask him if he can listen to the letters you wrote without interrupting and tell him that he can have a chance to speak at the end with any feelings, thoughts, or questions. Once he agrees, I will call on you one at a time. I will decide the order you'll read, depending on how he is absorbing everything. I may ask one or more of you to leave the room and wait outside, if he seems triggered in any way. If you're speaking and you see me put my hand on my heart, I'm reminding you to stay grounded and speak from your heart. Remember, crying is good and expected, so don't apologize for being emotional. Lastly, if he interrupts you or asks questions, just pause. I will address the question and let you know when to begin reading again. Just watch me for cues if you are unsure what to do, I am here to support all of you. The intervention is really an opportunity for all of you to say how you feel and to do something beautiful and loving for William."

We caravan over to William's house. Standing at the door, I can sense everyone is really nervous. I turn around and ask them all to take some deep breaths. I remind them we are here today as allies, filled with light and love, and that he will feel that if we remain present with our purpose. We ring the doorbell. No response. One more time. We see his car in the driveway, so we know he is home. Dad has a key, but before I have him open the door I ask if they believe he has any weapons in the house. I have security with me, but it's best not to take any chances.

"No, definitely not," they assure me. "He has never been violent."

I gesture to Dad to unlock the door. As we enter, Dad heads straight to William's bedroom, as we discussed. The rest of us head to the living room. I can see how bad things are just by looking at the house, which shows signs of months of hoarding. The kitchen is strewn with pots, pans, takeout boxes, empty jars, and trash. Nothing has been put away—or thrown away. There is not a speck of countertop to be seen. The living room is piled high with papers, and there is not an open seat to be had. We begin clearing off the chairs and the sofa, but there is not enough room for me to sit down so I remain standing for the next hour.

"Hi, William," I say when he enters the room. "I'm Elisa. Your family has been worried about you. They asked me to come help talk to you about some of their fears and concerns. They've prepared some letters they want to read to you. Are you willing to listen? They worked really hard on them."

William nods yes. "Is this an intervention?" he asks.

"Yes," I say. "But we are going to go really slow and just let them talk about their feelings. Then when they're done you can ask me any questions or talk about how you feel. Good?"

He doesn't say anything, just looks down at his lap where his cat has just settled.

"Okay then," I begin. "Mom, why don't you start." Immediately her tears come and William reaches for her hand, and I know we are going to be okay. William is able to be present, and he clearly cares about them. I make my way through his sister and brother, deciding the order by carefully watching William. I never take my eyes off of him, as I'm looking to see what is registering and what's not. Where he seems uninterested, when shame or fear seem to take over. His subtle movements, the color of his skin, the pace of his breathing, whether he is sweating or shaking—all signs letting me know somatically how he is doing without ever saying a word. He continues to stroke the cat, which is keeping him calm and grounded.

Toward the end of the last letter, I see something out of the corner of my eye: a little dark spot scurrying across the floor. I want to scream but I hold it in. Dad is the last to go, and he's reading his asks and everyone is crying. I refuse to let my aversion to mice ruin this important moment.

"Thank you all so much for sharing," I say. "That was beautiful. William, I heard so much love in those letters. Could you feel it too?"

"I guess," he says. "Where am I going?" Another good sign: he seems willing to go to treatment.

"Well, my colleague Chris is outside. He's going to drive you to the treatment center. Would you like to meet him?"

"Okay," he says. "I need a cigarette, is that okay?"

"Of course," I say. "I will walk you out and introduce you." I motion for his family to stay put as William and I walk back through the overflowing kitchen and out the front door.

As I walk back in, the whole family gathers around me.

Now what? He didn't say anything. Is that bad? Is he okay? What should we do about the house? Can we spend some time together before he leaves?

"He is going to the treatment center, and that's all this day is about," I say. "Your work here is done, and it's time for you to go. We got this. I will call you once he's on the road. You all did amazing. We're not going to talk about anything else right now with him, we're going to give him the dignity of taking these next big steps on his own."

I walk them out to where William is finishing his cigarette. The family says their good-byes, and Mom hugs William. Chris glides him quickly into the house to pack a bag.

Fifteen minutes later, Chris and William come out with his bag in tow. I stop William and look him straight in the eyes.

"I am so proud of you, William," I say. "This is one of the most courageous things you could do for yourself. You never have to feel the way you do today ever again. Your family is amazing. I have been working with them for a month now. If you're up for it, I would love to work with you, too. I'll have your back the entire way. It is my job to be your educator and advocate. I will speak to you over the next few days and come and see you soon. You are a special person, and I can't wait to meet you when you become the guy again they all spoke about today." He hugs me and gets into the car, and Chris drives him toward the next stop on his soul's journey.

⸻

THE DAY AFTER I tell my bosses I am retiring from the entertainment business, I am busy in my office, calling clients and colleagues to let them know about my decision. With each call I'm letting go a bit more of this chapter of my life. I'm already starting to relax and feel more myself than I have in years. I've had my smile back for less than twenty-four hours

SOULBRIETY

when my assistant yells from the hallway, *Sally Beck on line 2!* and I feel the blood drain out of my body. Sally Beck is the queen of immediate information. She provides an up-to-the-minute news source online, reporting who had been hired, which scripts had just been bought, which director had just signed onto an anticipated film, and perhaps most infamously who had walked off set, gotten a DUI, or been fired. The effect she'd had on the agenting community could not be underestimated, putting us on the defensive with every piece of information that might impact a client. We had to get to that client immediately, day or night, lest they read the information from Sally first. While she no doubt intended to provide a service to the industry, her sharp tongue—combined with her uncanny ability to infuse gossip into any piece she wrote—made her more feared than loved. While everyone in Hollywood eagerly read it, no one wanted to be part of the train wreck people were coming to the blog to see.

"Hi, Sally," I said.

"I'm writing it," she says. "And I have some questions."

"Please, Sally, I just want a quiet exit," I almost beg. "No drama, no meanness, okay?"

"Listen, once a year I write a feel-good piece," she says. "This will be that piece. Now answer the questions. First one, what the fuck is your name? Is it Elisa or Lisa?" It's literally the last thing I expect her to ask, but it turns out to be the most meaningful.

"Elisa is my real name," I tell her, recounting how I changed to Lisa in college to make it easier on people. "By the time I got promoted as an agent there was only Lisa Hallerman." In truth, right after I'd gotten sober I'd gone to my boss and told him I was changing my name back to Elisa.

"No, that would be too confusing. Everyone knows you as Lisa. Don't make it such a big deal—it's only a nickname," he said. And so it never happened.

"Well," she says, "from now on you are Elisa. Let's get to why you decided to leave the biz and where you're going!" I spend the next fifteen minutes explaining how I came to the decision, how I felt my calling had shifted to addiction recovery services, and my vision for the future.

"Time to let go of the old," Sally says as we finish up the call. "Best of luck, Elisa."

That phrase "time to let go of the old" sticks with me. In a way I'm actually doing the opposite: I'm returning to a part of myself I've somehow left behind. Yes, I want to achieve new things. I want to try out new ideas. But I also want to feel like *myself* again. I realize I've lost contact with who I know myself to be in the last few years. I'm ready to reclaim my character and essence, and take off the mask I have been wearing for all this time.

I've taken great care with the sober living home, filling it with furnishings that, while masculine, also feel like "me." I've picked out every dish and every chair, paying for everything out of my savings account. I am focused solely on creating a home where these men can heal. By now we have nine beds, and all of them are full. I don't live at the house, but I have an office downstairs where I meet with our clients for counseling sessions. When I ask how they're doing, they invariably launch into complaints or questions. *The other guys in the house suck. When can I have my phone back? How long un-til I can spend the night with my girlfriend at her house?* But on rare occasions, one of the guys gets vulnerable and wants to talk. Then I start to hear the stories of how they ended up here, what happened along the way. I love these conversa-tions, insatiably curious about what lies beneath each man's addiction.

Pretty early on I get a referral from a family friend. His son, Flynn, is just coming out of inpatient rehab and needs a sober living environment. Flynn is twenty-two, and I've known him his whole life. We both know without a doubt that he's an addict, but he's not quite ready for the commitment to sobriety. One morning he texts that he's moving out of the sober living house, which terrifies me. Without sobriety he won't be able to do the soul-level healing he desperately needs, and I'm afraid of what will happen to him if he doesn't get help. So I head over to the house to find him. I'm waiting in the living room when he gets home to pack his things. I look up as four guys walk into the room. It's Flynn and three strangers, who by the looks of them have been living a rough life on the streets. They also look to be more than twice Flynn's age.

"Flynn, I'm sorry but these gentlemen cannot come into the house," I say. We have a rule that only the clients them-selves are allowed in the sober living home.

"They are my good friends!" Flynn protests.

"Your friends?" I ask. "When did you meet them?"

"I'm going to live with them," he says.

"Flynn, you have no money. How will you live?"

"I've got everything I need to make money right here," he says, defiantly holding up his phone. "Am I right guys?" One of his "good friends" gestures as if he is shooting a needle into his arm. Without hesitation I get up from the couch and grab the phone out of Flynn's dirty, sticky hand, walk to the bathroom, and toss it in the toilet. "My phone! My phone!" Flynn is screaming. "Why did you do that?!"

"I can't stop you from leaving the house," I say. "But you are *not* selling drugs." Flynn storms out.

He calls from a stranger's phone thirty-six hours later, asking to come back. *Thank god.*

It takes a few months and a dozen similar experiences for me to recognize what I've become in starting this sober living: a mom to nine twenty-something guys. Turns out, running a sober living home is about much more than just providing a sober place to live, get drug tested, and have house meetings. It's about helping manage the transition from an old lifestyle to a new one, and in my particular case, about helping boys grow up into men.

Among other things, this means teaching them a skill they may never have learned before: housekeeping. The sink seems to always be filled with dishes, coffee cups, and silverware, even though there's a perfectly good dishwasher sitting empty. Every day I arrive to a messier kitchen than the day before. I stare at the dishes, remembering the care I took to pick them out, the thought I put into each mug and fork. I have to laugh at what I didn't know back then: how most of our guys spent their adolescent years using, rather than doing household chores. They couldn't possibly appreciate the dumb dishes or coffee mugs the way I wanted them to; they just expected the house would have what they needed. One morning I get to a breaking point. *Time for a lesson*, I think. I gather up all the dishes, silverware, glasses, and mugs—both clean and dirty—and walk them out to my truck. I drive away without mentioning what I am doing, even to the staff.

The texts start coming in a few minutes later.

The dishes are gone!!!!

How can I eat without silverware?

There is nothing to drink from!!!

I ignore them. Later I hear they got creative, going to McDonalds across the street and taking plastic forks and used soft drink cups for their coffee. It takes about a week before I get the apology texts.

Sorry we get it now can we have the dishes back?

I promise we'll use the dishwasher if you'll just bring back the silverware.

Well, I think, *this is a good start.* But being a house mom is not really what I want to be doing. I am more interested in the inner work these young men need, figuring out what's underneath the using. I'm like a detective, always drilling down to find the source of their pain and which therapies are or aren't working and what doesn't make sense in the stories they're telling me.

And a lot doesn't make sense. The more I understand about addiction treatment, the more complicated it gets. The clinical treatment options are not regulated, and the only guidelines enforced are those the insurance companies require in order to reimburse your expenses. This means my clients are receiving care in a wide variety of clinicians and outpatient settings, some of which seem to be working while others definitely do not. Almost all of them have been in some sort of residential treatment or wilderness therapy program before they come to me. The role of the house is to provide oversight and a sober environment as they "step down" their care, a safe place to live while they complete outpatient treatment three to five days a week. But the types of treatment they're getting run the gamut. Some are working with drug and alcohol counselors, a certification requiring less education than getting a specific type of degree in psychology. Others are working with trained and licensed therapists, each of whom has their own methodology and treatment focus. I begin really listening to my clients and their families, to what they feel is working and not working. If something doesn't feel right to them about their therapist or treatment program, I ask a million questions. I also speak to the professionals my clients are working with, asking why they chose a particular methodology or treatment program for that particular client.

My main takeaway is that I don't know enough to really help. Not yet. I can tell that some clinicians and programs are better than others, but I am not remotely qualified to assess which would be right for a particular patient, especially one who has co-occurring mental health disorders. But I notice I *want* to understand—very much. I want to learn about the cutting-edge treatments, and to understand this word *trauma* and which types of treatment are trauma focused. My curiosity seems to be coming from a deeper place inside of me than just my mind. It's as if my heart itself is yearning for more information. Soon, it starts whispering to me about graduate school.

Getting licensed as a therapist or social worker would be a logical choice, but neither truly fits what I want to do. The problem is, I can't yet articulate what it *is* that I want to do. I just have a feeling that there's room in the field for something new, and I want to create it. So I need a grad program that has space for this vision to emerge. I need to learn everything from counseling to crisis intervention to addiction services to life management. I settle on a masters in psychology, which is broad enough to include all of the areas that interest me.

As I research programs, however, the syllabi I'm seeing don't interest me in the slightest. They are clinical programs preparing students for licensure as marriage and family therapists, social workers, or doctoral-level clinical psychologists. But the role of "therapist" is not calling to me. I want to focus on consulting and management in the field of mental health. Having now worked in addiction for two years, I see that nobody is offering cutting-edge client education and advocacy. The world of inpatient treatment is constantly changing, and the journey of recovery needs to be carefully tailored to the individual person's needs. It starts with picking the right treatment center, which goes beyond location. What treatment methodologies are they using? Which therapists will be available for the client's length of stay? Will the family program be robust enough for this particular client's needs? Common upheavals like turnover in clinical staff, new treatment research, and corporate buyouts of once-private centers mean that a center that may have been a good idea a few years back might be a really bad choice today—but how is a client to know that? And what is a client to do if a particular treatment format or focus doesn't work out as planned? I have a hunch someone like me could fill that knowledge gap.

What's more, while I want to understand psychology, I also want to learn about neuroscience, the body, philosophy, and soul. I have gone on to read more books by the philosopher James Hillman, whose book *The Soul's Code* my friend Zoe had recommended to me. His books lead me to Thomas Moore, who wrote *Care of the Soul* and *Dark Nights of the Soul,* among others. In doing some fan-girl research, I discover that James Hillman has been a psychologist on faculty for Pacifica Graduate School—just up the coast from me in Santa Barbara—and that Thomas Moore has held many lectures there as well. As I start researching Pacifica, I see that their curriculum couldn't be more different from the other schools I'm looking at, in an exciting way. Specifically, they offer a five-year masters/Ph.D. program in "depth psychology with an emphasis on somatic studies." I don't even know what this means, but something resonates for me. So I pore over the website, reading every page and watching every video. Moment by moment, I feel my heart opening. I also feel a connection I'm not expecting: Pacifica's program is based on the work of the psychologist Dr. Carl Gustav Jung, whose name I know from many years in Alcoholics Anonymous.

In 1931, Jung was treating an alcoholic named Rowland H. at his clinic in Switzerland. After working together tirelessly, Rowland relapsed. In his greatest despair, he returned to Dr. Jung asking if there was any hope at all for him. Jung told him that further medical or psychological treatment would not be effective at this point and that without a "vital spiritual experience" he had little chance of getting well. Rowland followed Jung's advice and sought out a religion-based recovery group. He found the Oxford Group, which offered a recovery program based on principles including self-discovery, amends, and service. In the early 1930s, many of the Oxford Group's members were able to get sober, including Rowland. As part of the Oxford program, Rowland went on to share his experience, strength, and hope with other struggling alcoholics. One of these men, Ebby T., got sober as a result. Ebby went on to bring sobriety to Bill Wilson, who would himself go on to found Alcoholics Anonymous in the United States. Years later, in 1961, Bill was able to thank Carl Jung himself. In their correspondence, Jung explained that he believed Rowland's craving "was the equivalent on a low level of the spiritual thirst of our being for wholeness." The centrality of the spiritual experience to AA was a direct influence from Jung, and now I have stumbled upon a graduate school devoted to depth psychology—also directly influenced by Jung's work. Something about it just feels right, too synchronistic to pass up. I decide to make the journey to Santa Barbara for the in-person information day.

After a gorgeous drive up the Pacific coast, I see a small sign that says *Pacifica Graduate School*. I turn onto a dirt road leading up a mountain, the road lined with the tallest, most gorgeous Moreton Bay Fig trees I've ever seen. There seem to be flowers everywhere, and I feel like I'm driving into a serene enchanted forest. Suddenly the hustle and bustle of LA feels a million miles away, replaced by a calm tranquility. I reach the campus to find it situated on the top of the mountain, with views for miles in every direction. The buildings are low profile, so the whole place just looks like *nature*. It's stunning. As I walk into the auditorium, I see beautiful tapestries hanging on the walls, alongside photos and quotes from psychologists James Hillman, Marion Woodman, and Carl Jung himself.

I take a seat and listen intently to the faculty presentation. Every topic they present is more exciting to me than the next:

the soul, dreams, trauma, neuroscience, the unconscious. I learn that Pacifica is the home to the archives of the great mythologist Joseph Campbell, best known for synthesizing the elements of dozens of cross-cultural myths into a universal Hero's Journey. I know from working in Hollywood just how much of an influence Campbell's map has had on American film—providing structure to such blockbuster movies as *Star Wars*, *The Matrix*, *Harry Potter*, and many others. I have never before considered the possibility that this mythic journey offers a deeper understanding of the journey of the human soul. I can't wait to learn more.

The first day of school I walk into a large classroom where my cohort is meeting for the first time. Instead of desks, I see a bunch of chairs set up in a circle and some comfy pillows and yoga blankets on the floor. I'm slightly taken aback by how weirdly casual it all seems. Law school this is not. But I'm still feeling good about the decision, and I start to meet my fellow students. As class begins, we are standing in a circle and our professor asks us to introduce ourselves.

"We'll go around the circle," she says. "Tell us your first name, and then do either a movement or make a sound that goes along with who you are." *Um, what?* I'm imagining all my Hollywood friends sitting in their offices, wheeling and dealing, getting ready to rush out to their one o'clock power lunches. But I decide to go with it. When it's my turn I say *Elisa* and do a little wiggle. The teacher stops.

"Did you say Lisa or Elisa?" she asks.

"Elisa," I reply, smiling inside.

I travel to Santa Barbara once a month and stay for four days. Most of the students stay in the campus dorms, but the first weekend I'm not quite ready to join the masses. Even though I've already paid for housing, I decide I would be more comfortable at a hotel. At 9 p.m. on day one, as the rest of the class is heading back to the dorms, I get in my car and drive to my nearby hotel. Going down the dark, windy hill from school, I begin to have a familiar disconnected feeling. I shrug it off and check into my hotel. The next morning I head back up to campus. As I walk into the dining room I see my classmates seated together at a few tables, laughing and enjoying breakfast. *I want this*, I think. *I want connection, and these people are my new community.* From that day on, I stay in the dorms. Yes, I upgrade to a private room with my own bathroom, but I'm there! I love our late night hangs and getting to know my new friends, who span in age from their 20s to their 60s.

I enrolled in Pacifica to earn a degree. What I didn't expect was to *heal*. To go deep with my cohort, sharing our innermost secrets, fears, and pain—and make it through to the other side. Pacifica becomes my home away from home; the classroom, my vessel for healing; my classmates, much-needed witnesses for my transformation and vice versa. Pacifica becomes a safe place where once a month for four days I feel nurtured, seen, heard, and held—as maybe I have never been before.

Month after month, I drive up the PCH to school and back again to Los Angeles. I cherish my time in the car, despite the fact that I hate to drive. The view of the ocean is profound and brings back so many memories. I am always inspired coming home from school. The dots of my past seem to finally connect. I begin to see meaning in my limitations and opportunities in my failures. I discover that what I've always wanted was to understand the deep in myself and others; I've always been insatiably curious about what lies beneath. I'm also realizing that I am not accessing this type of depth with the clients at the sober living home, as the day-to-day operations are more than a full-time job in themselves. I make the difficult decision to close the house.

As I decide what to do next, I think about what I really enjoy in owning the sober house. I love managing the clients' lives in early recovery, evaluating their growth and making adjustments to their short- and long-term treatment plans, incorporating family treatment for the entire system, and bringing in more holistic care that addresses core issues rather than just symptoms. I also love working with brand-new clients, to help them understand the treatment landscape and decide which direction would be right for them. I'm always reaching out to the authors of the books I'm reading in school, thanking them for their insight and in a few instances, taking them out to dinner. Some of this feels new, but much of it feels . . . familiar. In fact, I'm doing what I used to do with my Hollywood clients. I'm curating the best of the best, creating relationships, and building a network of friends and advisors I can consult when I need advice or information. The more I try to put away the "agent" in me, the louder she seems to get. I realize that leaving the entertainment industry was one thing, but I was a great agent because that's who I am on the inside. Excited by this awareness, I begin to create a vision of my own agency—a *recovery* agency.

I know that trusting soul—and listening to other souls who know more than I do—will guide me down the right path, one that is helpful to others and true to myself. For the first time in my life I know I'm building a career I can be completely faithful to. Thanks to the difficulties of my personal history, I find I'm easily able to deal with the conflict, disappointment, and fear that come with the addiction recovery process. I believe I am ready to face all the challenges that will come my way. But of course, soul isn't done with me. It's always just when we are getting a bit cocky and think we've found the magic elixir that soul steps in to remind us there is more to learn. I have no idea that all the healing I've been doing in school has only brought me closer to my greatest trial: facing the monster of my unhealed trauma, lurking just around the corner.

CHAPTER TEN

The Inmost Cave

Although it's on silent mode because I'm in class, my phone is always sitting beside me. So I can see that Caroline is calling me, and it makes me smile. After almost two months in intensive, focused trauma treatment, she's gotten back her phone privileges. I'm proud of her, but I don't have time to really think about it; I'm typing a mile a minute to capture every detail of what my professor is saying.

After class I eat my lunch outside with my classmates, enjoying the fresh air. I love being outside at Pacifica. I love the views, the scent of the flowers all around, the birds chirping nonstop from the trees. Reluctantly I excuse myself to make a few business calls. I'm suddenly running a recovery agency, after all. I take full advantage of the breaks in our 8 a.m.-to-8 p.m. school day, checking on my clients and their clinical teams, doctors, lawyers, and family members.

After properly sorting my cup, plate, and silverware into the appropriate wash tubs, I grab coffee and a snack for later before heading back out to the gardens. I find a seat on a bench and press redial, ready to congratulate Caroline on having gotten her phone back. But before I can say a word, she starts yelling.

"I *hate* this place!" she says. She's out of breath and has clearly been crying. "Everyone hates me. I suck at treatment! It's pointless. Why did I think this time would be any different? I'm not going back. Don't even try. I'm too embarrassed. It would be humiliating to walk back in there. I won't do it."

Now I'm starting to get the picture. She has left treatment.

"Where are you?" I ask.

"I'm walking to the bus stop," she huffs. "I already have my bags. They seemed *happy* to have me leave and just gave me my stuff when I asked for it."

"It must be so cold outside," I say, picturing her trudging through the snow. "How are you managing your bag?" Secretly, I'm trying to just calm her down by getting her to talk about her surroundings. I'm not going to talk about going back; instead I want to try and get her out of the thought loop that's holding her hostage.

That her nervous system is in flight mode, and her fear is ruling her behavior isn't a surprise to me. She's been struggling like this for years. She suffers intense mood swings, self-hatred, risky and reckless behavior, suicidal ideation, depression, and dissociation, to name a few. Even though she's been given a deferred diagnosis of borderline personality disorder, I believe her primary issue is unresolved trauma from the past. But we can't really know, since she's too early in sobriety to definitively say whether it's a mood or personality disorder or underlying trauma—the symptoms of mood/personality disorders and underlying trauma can look identical. But somehow Caroline's trauma has gotten triggered today, and she is fleeing treatment to escape the intense feeling that something undesirable and excruciatingly painful is happening to her. It's my job to help her see, eventually, that the pain isn't happening to her in the present; what she's feeling is a reactivation of terrible feelings from the past. But now is not the time for that.

"What happened today?" I ask, hoping she'll give me a glimpse of whatever triggered her to leave.

"Nothing happened," she says. I can hear her trying to catch her breath from crying, carrying her suitcase, and the freezing cold air outside. "I just can't do this, Elisa, treatment doesn't work for me. I'm damaged. I'm beyond help. I'm a bad seed. Please let me go! I don't know why you bother caring about me at all. Pretty much everyone else hates me and thinks I'm a piece of shit."

With every sentence out of her mouth, what she is really telling me is, *I am stuck in my shame.* We feel guilt when we have done something bad; we feel shame when we believe we *are* bad. Guilt can be useful, as it provides clues that we may have misstepped and should consider trying to repair and make amends for our behavior. But shame is never useful, especially for trauma survivors. Over and over I've seen the shame of "what happened" become a toxic spiral leading to depression and anxiety disorders. This is Caroline's pattern, and the way she copes with the intensely painful feelings is to get angry. Feeling rage means she doesn't have to feel the full weight of the shame. I know where the shame is coming from, thanks to a text her group therapist just sent me. In this morning's session, right before Caroline walked out, she had hinted to the group that she'd been sexually abused as a young child. This does not surprise me, given her symptoms. But she has never directly spoken to me about it. It's been a ticking time bomb waiting deep inside her soul. If we cannot begin to carefully, gently, heal her pain, it will show up disguised as many other disorders for years to come.

"Well, I don't think you're a piece of shit. And I will continue to care about you until you can care about yourself," I say.

"I can't go back, I can't go back," she yells into the phone. "You don't understand. When I am there I feel totally helpless."

Okay, now we're making some headway; she's starting to let me in. I've been working with Caroline for a few years and we've finally built a relationship where she trusts me enough to reveal herself. For the first year or two, she couldn't let me in. She had to be constantly moving or getting out of wherever she was in effort to feel okay. But the chaos of her life was killing her, and over time she's started leaning on me. Like today; she didn't have to call me when she left, but she did.

"I'm not going back, Elisa. I can't."

"Okay," I say. "Let's just talk. How are you feeling right now?"

"I'm scared. I'm scared." She is crying again.

"What else?" I ask her.

"I'm afraid of everything."

"What else?"

"I am disgusting and I hate myself," she says, sobbing. I take a deep breath.

"I'm right here," I remind her. "It's just me and you on the phone. Just yesterday when I spoke to you, you were excited to be moving forward with your healing, getting more privileges and even starting to make friends." She starts to cry a little harder. I wait.

"What happened today?" I ask again, hoping she'll volunteer information about the sexual abuse her therapist mentioned.

"We did a psychodrama group. I wasn't the one sharing, but this guy was and he was confronting his stepsister. She was older and she molested him when he was really little."

"Wow, it must have been really hard to witness someone suffering from that kind of pain," I say. Caroline doesn't reply. "What happened in your body as you watched the process?"

"I got sick to my stomach," she says quietly. "I ran to the bathroom to throw up. Then I excused myself to my room to lie down. But I couldn't even lie down, I was frozen. I just stood there in my room looking out the window, and I knew I had to leave. So I packed up my stuff and then went to get my phone from the staff, and then I walked out the door and now I'm outside freezing and talking to you."

"Caroline, do you have any hunch what made you throw up?" I ask. "You don't have to reveal it to me. But do you know?"

"Yes, I know," she says after a long pause. "But I can't go there, Elisa! I'm so scared. My family will hate me." She starts to cry hard again.

"Caroline, you didn't do anything wrong," I assure her. "Whatever it was, it wasn't your fault. Your family loves you and they will understand."

"No, they won't!" she says, anger flaring up through the tears. "My parents didn't help me! I *told* them when it happened! And they believed my uncle's story, they didn't listen to me!"

Even though she's feeling intense pain and fear, it is very good news that she's sharing this with me. Just now I get a second text from her therapist, letting me know she and a colleague are pulling up to the bus station where Caroline is waiting.

"Go back to treatment, Caroline," I urge her. "You're so close. If you can face this, you can heal. I am right here for you. I am so proud of your resilience. Your adversity will become your strength and your superpower."

Caroline agrees to go back. I say good-bye, but Caroline interrupts.

"Elisa," she says. "Thank you for always being there. For believing in me even when I don't."

"I do believe in you," I tell her. "And I will always be here."

———

IT'S SUMMERTIME, AND my graduate program will end in January. I'm currently writing my Ph.D. concept paper—a summary explaining what my dissertation question is and how I plan to go about doing the research. All I know at this point is that my dissertation is about soul and addiction. I'm very curious about how soul might bridge the wide gap between the addiction treatment and trauma-focused treatment. I want to know if there's some way to bring them together, and I think the answer may be soul work.

That said, I'm confused about the "how" myself. The paper doesn't make much sense, even to me. I can sense that my dissertation chair doesn't like the first draft, but I keep pushing through. I'm determined to get it right.

Needing a break from writing, I head to the East Coast for the Fourth of July and a little girls' getaway weekend with my sister. We are headed to Montauk for the weekend. We get to our hotel, and the open-air lobby is a sea of city dwellers already drinking and having fun. We check in, have a walk around the grounds with our pups, take a shower, and head to the hotel restaurant. After dinner, I am walking around the grounds when I suddenly trip and go flying face-first off a ledge, landing hard on the ground. It's dark and crowded, and I hadn't realized I was walking across some sort of stage. I'm probably the only one in the whole place who hasn't had a drink, yet there I am lying on the ground. The minute I land, I know something is terribly wrong with my arm. I'm holding it to make sure it doesn't fall off. A crowd gathers around me, and I see my sister pushing through trying to get to me. I am a klutz on my best day, so she has no way of knowing the severity of my injury. She attempts to walk me back to the room, but I faint from the pain before we get there. Next thing I know, I'm in an ambulance. I'm in so much pain my body is literally shaking, so the medics are trying to determine if I hit my head.

"No," I say. "This is my body's natural response to trauma." With that, my sister—who is sitting in the ambulance with me—is no longer as worried. *If you could lecture the EMTs on trauma*, she tells me later, *I knew you would be fine*. By the end of the weekend, it has been confirmed I've broken the radial head in my right elbow and need surgery.

A metal plate and a bunch of screws later, I'm sent home with a ton of opiates and my right arm immobilized. For the next nine months I have to do intense physical therapy to regain my normal range of motion. So you guessed it, no concept paper happening.

As if the broken elbow isn't enough, I'm now faced with a week of detox from the pain medication I was only taking for two weeks. As opiates were never my drug of choice, I've never experienced this type of withdrawal. My skin is crawling, my legs are cramping and restless, my body is either shaking with chills or sweating profusely. I can't sleep and my stomach is cramped and constipated. I feel like I've been run over by a truck. I thought I understood my opiate-addicted clients, but I have a new understanding. Getting clean forces the impossible choice: kick the opiates and suffer this sickness, or keep using in hopes of postponing the pain a little bit longer.

The next few months I stay in Connecticut, living with my sister and her family. I spend time with my niece and nephew and work on getting my strength back. I stop writing and really have quiet time again. But as anyone who has recovered from an accident or illness understands, being forced into stillness has a way of bringing old, festering wounds to the surface. While I've done a tremendous amount of personal growth work over the years, there are demons I still have to face. Losing use of my dominant hand is frustrating to say the least, and the physical pain of the injury is making me depressed. Returning to live with family will throw even the most stoic back into painful familial roles. What's worse, I'm uncomfortably dependent. My food needs to be cut for me, and I need assistance in the bathtub to help me wash my hair.

I often use an exercise called the "balance wheel" to help my clients check in on where they are in their lives. I use "lives" in the plural, as each of us has many different areas within our life. I draw a pie chart with eight parts: work, school, play, spirituality, family, friends, romantic partner, and wellness. Then I have the client tell me how much time they're spending on each part. Usually a few will be more heavily occupied than others, but when we are living in just one area—as I presently am, with all of my attention focused on physical wellness—we begin to feel very off balance. It's easier for me to see this in my clients than in myself. But later down the line I will look back at this time and see that I was ripe for an even bigger healing. And that's exactly what I get. No sooner has my external injury begun to heal than some of my older inner soul wounds—which have been needing reconciliation for many years—rise to the surface in such a painful and dramatic way that they can no longer be ignored.

At Pacifica I was fascinated with what philosopher and religious scholar Henry Corbin named "the imaginal." A proponent of a creative version of spirituality, Corbin believed in a soul realm where archetypes and individual mythical figures dwell. Contrary to the "made-up" world associated with the word "imaginary," he saw the *imaginal* as a very real part of every human's inner world. The imaginal space provides a gateway into soul—an entry point for exploring and understanding our complicated emotions so we can be consciously inspired by them instead of unconsciously ruled by them. Among other methods, the practice of personification grew out of Corbin's work, imagining from the heart.

In the long days of my recovery, I turn to this wellspring as a lifeline. Framed as aspects of the imaginal realm, I can relate to mythology, dreams, storytelling, images, and archetypes not just as fanciful ideas but as aids in creation, growth, and healing. Through writing, creative visualization, meditation, art, and time in nature, I begin to create relationships with my own internal chaperones, the parts of myself who behave in certain ways and influence how I perceive the outside world. I already know Trixie, who is my addiction personified. My recent brush with opioids underscores how important it is for me to maintain a relationship with her. Trixie is always trying to convince me of something, so I know she's operating when my thoughts become persuasive and repetitive. She keeps saying the same thing over and over again, despite the fact that I have already said no. In the past I would finally relent, just to get her to quiet down—holding a boundary took more energy than I had. But today I recognize what's happening as it happens. I acknowledge that Trixie is the one speaking, and I am able to dialogue with her by asking *why*. Why is she so insistent right now? Usually the answer I get has something to do with isolation, stress, and fear. Maybe I've been alone in my head for too many days in a row, and I need to check in with my sober community. Or maybe I haven't done enough self-care, letting work take over every minute of my life. Or maybe I've been feeling sorry for myself, and I need to set a boundary and tap into my inner strength. Once I understand her motivation for wanting to numb out, go dark, and not feel, I know what I need to look at in order to meet her need in a healthier way.

Without an enormous amount of respect for Trixie—allowing her voice to be heard and acknowledged—I run the risk of falling back into unconscious addiction behaviors. But by listening to her, I learn what she has to teach me, and together we can make better decisions.

As I spend each afternoon meditating, letting my attention roam across the inner planes, I become aware of another strong character dwelling in my consciousness. Her name is Gwen, and her job—I can suddenly see—has been to feed me stories about my weakness and my need for a savior. Outside of my awareness, and for many decades, Gwen has been vigilantly reminding me that I am not strong enough or well enough to survive on my own. That I need support I am not getting, and—most importantly—that I need someone to come take care of me. She is quick to remind me of all the times I have been emotionally or financially abandoned in my life and left to fend for myself. She keeps me small and my voice muted, out of protection. And she has never been louder than in the days since the accident. I already feel vulnerable and weak, and she is trying to send me into a flying panic about it. Luckily, I understand her role now. So instead of falling for it, I do a visualization. I invite all the personas inside of me who have something to say to show up in a circle, not unlike a twelve-step meeting. One by one, I allow each part of me to share what's going on for her. Today's participants are Trixie, Gwen, Short Pants, and Flossy. I first met Short Pants when I was an assistant in Hollywood and was working for an egocentric and most likely narcissistic boss. In his ongoing effort to make me doubt myself—so he could maintain his superiority—he would regularly remind me that I was "still in short pants." It felt insulting, even though I didn't know what the phrase meant. When I looked it up I discovered that saying someone is "in short pants" means they are still a child, not yet ready to wear the full-length pants of a man. So my hunch was right: it was, in fact, an insult—meant to shame me into feeling insecure, immature, and inexperienced. So my friend Short Pants holds the shame of being not good enough and sees the world through those eyes.

Flossy, conversely, is my biggest cheerleader. She is fierce, bold, determined, unapologetic about who she is and confident in her ability to do hard things. After listening to everyone share, I realize that Trixie, Short Pants, and Gwen have been taking turns in the driver's seat of my psyche. Not great choices, any of them. So I thank them for sharing, turn down their volume, and send them to the back of the van. Elisa takes the driver's seat again and I keep Flossy seated shotgun as my upbeat sidekick. While it takes vigilance to keep her there—and the others in the back—just becoming aware that I have someone on my team helps me turn a corner.

＝

BEYOND THE PHYSICAL healing, I've also reconnected to my soul. I've started to deliberately care for my inner world and to integrate the wisdom I learned from the accident. In doing so, I've become more *me*. This is not to imply that I have it all figured out or I am "fixed." Actually, it's the opposite: this integration has required me to become willing to face more parts of myself, including the dark ones. One of the most obvious imperfections I've had to encounter is the way in which I have chosen to be in a relationship with a married man, someone who causes me more pain than joy. I make a commitment to myself to end the affair.

When we met, I was still grieving Andy's death and Scott's marriage. I had no one playing the role of savior in my life, a role that had always been filled by a man. Even though we were just friends, Jimmy stepped into those shoes with ease. He was always there to comfort me, make me laugh, and tell me everything was going to be okay. By the time he began pursuing me romantically, I was already so attached to him I believed this *had* to be love. I went into it willingly, knowing that it was not the right thing to do. It was dishonest, but somehow I convinced myself that I *needed* Jimmy. Looking back, I see I still had trauma I hadn't worked through, and in spite of having been sober, I didn't love myself enough to believe I deserved a healthy relationship. And this relationship was not healthy.

At the beginning, Jimmy showered me with attention. But as time went on, the experience shifted. I found I was often confused, feeling like I was getting mixed messages and half-truths. It seemed as if I was always to blame for miscommunications. I wondered at times if I was going crazy. But by that point my self-worth was so entangled in the affair, I couldn't imagine how I could get out of it. So I told myself it would all work out somehow; I just had to stick it out.

No matter how painful it was—and it got very, very painful—I did just that. I always went back to believing he was the hero, never letting him stay the villain for too long. I became dependent on the ups and downs of oxytocin and cortisol that came with being "in" and "out" of favor with Jimmy. Soon a familiar addict feeling took over, even though it was destroying me. I often felt worn down by mixed messages that made me feel as if I had to prove myself. My soul knew better, but I kept her quiet. I was drowning in toxicity and more trauma, but I was unable to break the bond.

Thankfully, my internal light is starting to flicker again now. I can no longer deny the call from soul. I'm ready to face this truth now, but I have literally no idea how to end the relationship for good. The best I can come up with is— you guessed it—to move. (I've done a lot of work but still haven't healed my pattern of "Get me the fuck out of here.") The timing seems perfect. I'll move back to Connecticut for the summer and live the beach lifestyle. I convince myself I am making a healthy choice to be closer to friends and family, rather than running away.

But even though we're now three thousand miles apart, Jimmy's pull remains strong. One weekend I plan a girls' getaway with some of my sober soul sisters. I try to be social, but Jimmy is calling constantly and has my head spinning. He's upset because he has a business trip in New York City and wants to meet up with me, but I'm committed to the beach weekend. He won't let up until I agree to leave early and come meet him. The girls decide we're going to pack a lunch and head to the beach for a little ocean therapy. I'm supposed to be putting on my bathing suit and packing my stuff. Instead, I'm in a screaming fight over the phone with Jimmy. He's going on and on about how he needs me right now, how he loves me, and how this is the perfect time for us to be together. Inside I know that if he really loved me, he would be supporting my choice to spend time with my friends. Instead he is going on about what shitty people my girlfriends are, how no one loves me the way he does, and that if I don't give him what he wants he will seek it elsewhere. Finally I hang up on him. I hear them calling me from downstairs to hurry up already. I race to pack my things and head to where my friends are all waiting for me. They can see the sadness written all over my face.

"You are acting like a drug addict," Gracie says as we walk toward the beach. "Needing something that is killing you at the same time. I hate seeing you this way."

"Don't you think that's a bit much?" I say, trying to downplay it. "Please just let me be. I don't want to talk about it."

Gracie stops walking and drops her bags on the sidewalk.

"We aren't going any further until you *do* want to talk about it," she says. "You're scaring me and all your friends. Look at yourself. You've turned into a shell of who you used to be. This relationship is destroying you."

Destroying me?

"I don't see it that way," I say angrily. "It's complicated. You just don't understand."

"Oh, I understand perfectly," Gracie says. "You are avoiding the inevitable and believe his every word even though his actions speak volumes. This isn't what love is. We are the ones that actually love and care about you. It's not okay that you don't trust yourself to do the things you are know are right and good for you. You always feel guilty. You don't even realize how this relationship isolates you from your friends."

I can't even cry; I am in pure defensive mode. My ego has come out in full force to protect me, and I am armored up and ready to take on the world in order not to feel these feelings.

Our other friends have caught up to us, and suddenly I feel ganged up on and misunderstood.

"What is this?" I say. "An intervention?"

"Sure, yes. It's an intervention," Gracie says. "You're in a damaging and corrupt relationship. Please let us get you help."

I'm shocked. This all seems so *extreme*.

"No," I push back. "I don't need your help. I'm not interested in your feedback." I grab my bags and head back to the rental house, trying to tell myself my friends are the problem. *They're out of line. They don't really understand.* I spend the rest of the day isolating in my room, boiling over with anger and resentment toward these so-called friends of mine.

But at the same time, there is a tiny voice whispering inside of me. *They are right*, it says. *I need help.* Desperately. They have named what I could not. Even in sobriety we make mistakes, sometimes big ones. We lose our way, steer down a slippery dangerous road, and fall out of integrity. If I want to survive, I need to slowly disentangle my roots from Jimmy's, allowing soul to grow down into my own soil again. But this transformation is going to ask a lot of me. It's a commitment I ask of my clients, so I know how hard it is. And I know I'm not ready to face the dark night that will be triggered if I exit this relationship. So as usual, Jimmy gets his way: I leave the trip early and head to the city.

Jimmy is now separated and seemingly headed for divorce. We talk about the future and begin to plan a vacation getaway. Yet there is something gnawing at me. I feel myself playing small in our interactions. As if I have to let him be in the spotlight and can't fully be myself. It's a familiar feeling, but I'm not yet ready to look it in the eye. I notice that while we're together my stomach is in knots. I have anxiety and some of my OCD behaviors are coming back. At the same time, I sense he is distracted and not fully engaged with me. My soul starts to ask probing questions. *Is this what you really want to feel in your relationship? Can you trust this man? You don't even like him anymore as a person, do you?* But like a phone call you know you're going to have to face eventually but want to put off as long as possible, I press "ignore" and carry on.

After a night out with friends, I am back at home. I am lying in bed when I start to get this funny feeling. I realize I haven't heard from Jimmy all day. In fact, he's only texted me—not called—for the last two days. My heart sinks. I immediately call Jimmy, who doesn't answer.

"What's up?" he texts.

"I want to talk to you, call me on Facetime?" I write.

As soon as I look into his eyes I know he is not alone. Wait, this *can't* be what is actually happening, can it? We had just discussed which headboard we wanted to buy.

"I'm wondering if there is something you're not telling me," I say, trying to remain calm. "Please just be honest."

"No, there's nothing," he says. "And why wouldn't I be honest?"

The conversation goes from bad to worse. Everything my friends were saying that day at the beach comes flooding back. While I pushed back that day, their words had never left me. As Jimmy continues to talk, I start to see and hear everything more clearly. I notice a convoluted and circular way the conversation is going despite me trying to remain in the facts of the situation. Is this what gaslighting feels like, I wonder? I'm starting to question my own reality. But I know what's going on. I can feel it in my gut. Finally I hang up. I'm too shocked to cry, too traumatized to speak. It's as if the ground has just collapsed underneath me.

The phone keeps ringing—it's Jimmy. I throw the phone across the room, trying to get it to stop. At first I ask myself over and over why he is doing this to me. But eventually soul breaks through, and I start to ask myself the *hard* questions. Why have I made these choices that are so out of alignment with who I know myself to be? Why have I stayed in this relationship, even though it's been killing me? I cannot pin all the blame on him. I chose to be part of a secretive, harmful relationship, and that's on me. I know I am not the first woman to be branded with the scarlet letter, nor the first to lose her way or her worth in exchange for a man's promises of love and protection. I'm not the first to give up her power and play by someone's else's rules—unaware of the warning signs and pretending things are fine even when her soul is screaming *no*. But I still have to face the repercussions, and my thoughts are a mess of self-recrimination. *I knew better. How could I let this happen? What was I thinking? I don't think I will ever forgive myself.*

Meanwhile the magnitude of the loss starts to sink in. For years Jimmy had been a close friend. I'd believed he would always have my back. The loss of his emotional support and friendship in my life is quick and profound. It drops me into the feelings of abandonment I've been trying to escape my whole life.

Over time, I see how I allowed Jimmy to claim the role of "hero" in my life from the day we met. Not because he truly loved me and wanted to be with me—like he said—but to maintain the power dynamic between us. At this point the only thing I can do is turn inward. Continue looking at my own contribution to this horrible situation and work on what still needs to be healed from long ago. If I'm going to find relief, answers, and explanations, I'm going to find it in soul.

Unlike the girl I'd been when I discovered my mom's addiction and my parents' affairs, or even the young woman I was when Andy committed suicide, today I have something to help cushion the fall. After many years of sobriety, trauma healing, and psychological study, I have *resilience*. I know how to do soul work. I know how to dive deep into the imaginal and sit with my feelings. I know how to find the courage to do the inner work. This wound is deep and linked to wounds from my past, as so much soul loss is, so it's not going to be a swift recovery. But I have patience and faith. I know healing will happen because I've climbed out of holes like this before. What's more, I no longer see crashes like this as entirely negative; I know that facing a dark night is profoundly healing. It's where we get to know ourselves at the deepest possible level.

I am shattered into tiny slivers, and I know the pieces will never fit back together in the same way. Instead, I have to undergo an alchemical transformation, becoming a different substance altogether. I know what I have to do: descend into the cave.

Back at Pacifica, I'd participated in an active meditation group. During the class we'd done a guided meditation to find our inner "cave." That first time, my cave felt like a terrifying abyss—the same abyss my nephew's soul had guided me out of the day I got sober. But in the years since, I've voluntarily returned to that cave over and over. Slowly, it has transformed into a place of healing and comfort, a place where I can retreat and do the soul work of healing.

So now, isolated in my house in Connecticut, I go back in. My imaginal cave is a safe haven in the underworld. The first time I went there, I pictured myself walking down a dark spiral staircase, feeling my way, no light to be seen. It felt scary but I knew I had no choice but to descend. Once I got to the bottom I could feel the walls cold and dripping with condensation. The whole place was cold and dark, which matched how I felt about myself.

Now, it looks a bit different. When I get to the spiral staircase today I see that it is lit with candles. Knowing I would return, I lit a candle for myself on each previous trip, until now every stair is glowing with light. As I enter the cave I notice that the floor is no longer cold; I've covered it with blankets and pillows that form a soft, protective cocoon I can snuggle into as I wait for the healing. There is no such thing as time in the cave. Healing happens fast on some days while on others I leave feeling more raw and ripped apart than when I entered. Each time I ascend the stairs I look behind and see pieces of myself lying among the pillows, not ready to be put back together. Waiting for the next descent, which will come in due time.

It is February and the dead of winter. My bedroom overlooks a frozen pond. There is no sign of life outside, only bare trees and a white sky. Everything outside is just as frozen as I feel inside. Some days I fear I won't ever recover, but one thing I know is that nature is always changing. I hold onto the metaphor of the seasons, knowing that as gloomy and lifeless as the pond looks today, there *will* be a day when the ice will melt and the ducks will come back. The trees will be green again, and the flowers will bloom. I know that I, too, will transform. This dark night will not last forever, even though it feels never ending. Each morning I get out of bed and open the curtains to see if that day is today. But no, the pond and I are still frozen.

I'm scared and grieving. Some days I want to rip my skin off, throw up, scream, cry, jump off a bridge, and hurt him—all at the same time. Thankfully my sobriety is deeply rooted; I never feel the urge to use drugs or drink. But I dearly want to escape the pain. My sister comes across the street and sits with me on the floor, her face worried.

"Is there anything I can do for you?" she asks.

Just be near me.

Just hold on to me.

Tell me it's going to be okay.

She does just this, every day, for months. I count a strengthened relationship with my sister as one of the unexpected gifts of this awful time. The willingness to walk beside someone through the desolate landscape of a dark night, not trying to make it better, just providing companionship for the journey—that is compassion. Compassion is love. I am learning what love looks like each day.

"Something new will be born out of this," I write in my journal. "Maybe my soul purpose is to continue to learn hard, tough lessons because then I can teach others what I have learned. I will not hold on to this resentment and I will not be broken forever. I will not lose sleep or cry much longer. I will write, I will create, I will build, I will grow down."

About a year after I'm released from this dark night, I am sitting at dinner with Abe, a friend who knows the details of the breakup well. He asks how I am doing.

"Really, how are you?" he asks.

"I'm better," I say. "I'm going to be ok. He almost killed me, but I survived."

"He did kill you, Hallerman," he says. At first it sounds harsh, but he is more right than he knows. Something in me died in this experience. A version of me that I had outgrown, that was ready to be transformed. It's what happens in any true dark night of the soul: when we finally do rise from the ashes, we rise as something completely new—a stronger, more whole, more healed version of ourselves. All that's left to do is to make a living amends to all those who were affected by living in integrity, being honest, and always working on my own healing. And by always practicing Soulbriety like my life is at stake—because it is.

———

AFTER A LONG road of healing, I am getting ready to celebrate a milestone: turning fifty. As horrendous as the previous year has been, I am so grateful to be crossing the threshold into the second half of my life with unhealed trauma firmly behind me. While a year ago I'd envisioned something really different for my birthday, today *feels* far better than I could have imagined back then. I feel like the strong, courageous warrior in a fairytale, who showed up for herself and walked through the pain to the other side. There were countless days when I cried to my friends and family that it was too hard, that I feared I would never get over the devastation. Days where the feelings felt too overwhelming and insurmountable to carry on. My saving grace was that I *knew* it was a dark night. I knew I had the responsibility—not just to myself but for all women everywhere—to go inward, learn the lessons, gain the wisdom, return with the elixir, and help others do the same. I was not the first person to be heartbroken, nor to feel shame and humiliation for veering away from my moral compass. I was not the first to be betrayed and commit betrayal, to be scared, to feel broken, or to feel alone. Even though some days I wanted to fall asleep and never wake up, I never forgot that that's not how Soulbriety works. Soulbriety is my way of living, and it got me through.

The morning of my birthday, I go down to the beach with my best friends—all of whom have been staying at my house at the beach. There, at the edge of the Long Island Sound, we do a ritual. Witnessed by a circle of women, I clear the pain of the years before and set intentions for the second half of my life. After the ceremony we sit on the beach telling stories and laughing until we cry tears of joy. That night I host a dinner party with friends and family whom I had pushed away for too many years. As some of my closest friends and family stand up and give speeches, I am reminded what true love is: a bond at the level of soul. I finally understand what it means to have true soulmates, companions walking alongside me who see and celebrate my essence. I am overwhelmed with gratitude that the scary, insurmountable feelings I'd been carrying have dissolved. I'm left energized like a spirited fireball—ready to stand tall, shine bright.

We can't know where we'll take a wrong turn in life, or where someone else's wrong turn will drastically change our own course. But these things happen. We will, at times, be burdened by misery, despair, and agony. When it happens, our first response is usually to try and understand how we got there. It's the brain's natural attempt to make sense of the trauma. *Why did he do that? Why did she try to ruin my life? Why am I losing my job? Why is my life a mess? Why did they die? Why can't I just move on? Why me?* But there is only one question that heals: *Am I willing to do what it takes to heal my soul from this rupture?* We must jump out of the other person's head because we'll never be able to make sense of someone else's actions. But if we refocus internally, we can find our way. Regardless of how we got to this moment of soul loss, we've been presented with the job of a lifetime: using the pain to grow down further into soul.

CHAPTER ELEVEN

Living Soulbriety

I have been invited out to a farm in Florida to see a former client. It's a gorgeous day and not too humid so I put the top down in the rental car, and I drive up the coast with the windows rolled down so I can smell the ocean and feel the warm sun on my arms. I have Barry White blasting in the car, which of course reminds me of Andy. I'm excited to see my client, though I'm not sure what to expect. He's been doing really well the last couple of years and has worked hard on his recovery. While we've stayed in touch via text, I haven't seen him in a long time. I pull onto a dirt road and follow it around to the barn. Just as I'm about to get out of the car, I see him—and I almost can't believe my eyes. He has filled out his once-skeletal frame. He has a huge smile on his face and looks unbelievably healthy. I walk over and give Billy a giant hug. Tears are streaming down both of our cheeks.

"You saved me, Elisa," he says. "Thank you for saving my life."

"No, you saved your own life," I correct him. "I just mapped out directions and a plan how to do it." He smiles, asks if I would like to take a walk around the property.

We walk through a canopy of beautiful oak trees with blue sky sneaking through the wispy leaves. There are miles of grass surrounded by wooden fences and small ponds of water. In the background I can see homes on the outskirts of the ranch property. The serene surroundings couldn't be more perfect—a far cry of some of the places we have been together.

"So," I say. "Tell me everything. How did you end up living here?"

"Well, first of all, I'm three years and three months sober," he says proudly. "And the reason I'm living here is that I'm learning how to train traumatized horses."

"What?!" I ask, truly surprised. I had expected Billy to end up going to graduate school, or maybe work in the mental health field—we'd talked about those options many times before. But horse training? It's totally unexpected.

"I know, it sounds random," he laughs. "But I got really into understanding trauma after we worked together. I thought about going to school to become a therapist, but then a horse trainer friend of mine offered me a job with his horses. As you know, our family has had horses my whole life, so it made sense immediately. I started out doing conventional training and then it seemed so obvious to bring my own trauma work into the mix."

"That's beautiful, Billy. I'm so happy and proud of you."

"Really, the way I think of it, the horses are just me at another point in my life," he says. "And I'm their Elisa!" I laugh at the thought.

"You are perfectly suited to be doing this, Billy," I say. "You're exactly where you're supposed to be, and everything you experienced—even the really hard stuff—got you here."

"Exactly," he agrees. "You always said that to me and you were right!"

"Ok, what else do I need to know about you?" I ask.

"Well," he says, looking suddenly sad. "I just broke up with my girlfriend of a year. It's one of the reasons I reached out to you."

He has my undivided attention now. My mind is going in a million directions—did the breakup cause a relapse? Is he thinking about using again?

"What happened? Are you okay?"

"Yes, actually I am doing really well," he says. "I mean, I'm sad because I loved her. But we were growing apart. She didn't want to move out here to the farm, and she was going out all the time with her friends. That's not what I want to do every night anymore."

"So you're okay then?" I ask one more time, just to make sure.

"Yeah, actually," he says. "More than okay. It's amazing because I would never have been able to deal with this years ago. But with everything I learned about soul in working with you, and all the life skills I got during that time, I knew just what to do. I knew I was in a dark night. I had to go inside and feel my feelings, and really ask myself what I needed. I started seeing my therapist again, too."

"Billy, I am so proud of you!" I say. "You are showing up for your pain, working through it and not numbing out. Bravo!"

I feel my heart exploding with joy for him. Not just because of how far he's come, and how happy he seems, but because I can see how much light is emanating from within him. He looks more confident and present in his body, in a way I haven't seen before. There is a sparkle in his eye, and I've never seen him laugh this much. Tears spring to my eyes every time he giggles.

These are the moments with my clients that I cherish the most: seeing them make it to the other side. They're the moments that make the hard times bearable, the moments that give me proof that people *can* heal from trauma and addiction.

"You have a big, beautiful life, Billy," I tell him as we head to the house to make lunch.

"Yep," he says. "Because I live in my Soulbriety."

AFTER TWO YEARS in Connecticut—and a lot of time spent in my inmost cave—I am ready to move back to LA. I find a cute little guest house, right in my old neighborhood, where I can stay while I look for something more permanent. But the soul of the world has other plans. No sooner do I land back in LA than we all hear a new word for the first time: Covid. Like a worldwide game of musical chairs—where someone unexpectedly hit the pause button and the song suddenly stopped—we're all forced to take a seat exactly where we are.

From my perspective as a recovery manager, Covid couldn't have come at a worse time. The opioid epidemic is at a fever pitch, and I'm dealing with its effects every day. Now with this unprecedented and anxiety-producing pandemic, I start to see an immediate increase in substance abuse, overdoses, depression, and suicide. The full effects of this mental health crisis will not be known for many years to come.

I feel at a loss to help so many people who are suffering. Slowly I begin to suffer, too—but luckily I can lean on my Soulbriety. The first thing I have to do is make sure my *sobriety* is solid, since I know everything falls apart if I am not diligent about my recovery. I quickly join two twelve-step meetings a week on Zoom and talk regularly with my sponsor and sober soul sisters. I FaceTime with friends and family so I can feel the soul connection that comes from looking people in the eyes. I take time each day to deeply feel all of the emotions washing through me.

Knowing that others are feeling the same isolation and discomfort as I am, I decide to start a Soulbriety Group. We meet each week on Zoom, the size of the group slowly increasing as we go. The group is for anyone who is suffering. There is a mix of recovering addicts, newly sober addicts, those in Al-Anon (a twelve-step program for the family and loved ones of addicts), women with eating disorders, others with mental health issues such as anxiety and depression. We start each meeting with a lesson on soul and then shares from the group. Each member of the circle is building their own Soulbriety Plan, week by week. Together we walk through grief of a lost loved one, a lost pet, a relapse, financial fear, a breakdown, illness, heartbreak, betrayal, and fear. I watch as each individual begins to integrate the learning they need from the dark night we're in. Side by side I watch them as they carry each other through, shining light for each other to see their way out of the dark. Watching their transformations I realize it's time to get this work into the world in a larger way. I start outlining a proposal for a book on Soulbriety, motivated to share the message of soul work with more people than I could ever reach with my business alone.

But as the days at home get longer, I start to feel sick. I have unexplainable pain throughout my body. In addition to the achiness, I feel restless and anxious. I chalk it up to being cooped up for so many months. I try to take more walks around the neighborhood and keep myself on a schedule, but something fundamental is off with me. I can't put my finger on it, and the symptoms mount but don't add up to any obvious diagnosis. My eyes are getting infected, and there are giant cysts on top of my lids that need to be surgically removed. I am dizzy and nauseous all the time. I develop terrible migraines and begin to take prescription medicine for them. I have days where I can't get any food down without getting sick, yet I am gaining weight and seem to be swollen in weird areas in my body. I keep calling my doctor and having telehealth appointments, but she doesn't see anything serious enough to warrant going to the hospital during a pandemic.

I begin to wonder if some of my symptoms might be somatic responses to anxiety and depression, not unlike the clients I'm speaking to everyday. I go back to the hallmarks of my Soulbriety. First, I look at the story of what is happening. In my journal I describe the key events that have happened in the past few months, the current relationships I am involved in, and where my discomfort is showing up in my body. Soon I see how many traumatic Post-it Notes have recently gotten added to my soul, so I reach out for assistance. I have come to learn that *assistance* is not the same as *help*. To someone like me, for whom self-sufficiency has been a survival mechanism, the word "help" has always felt victim-y, like I'm some damsel waiting to be rescued—a mindset I'd abandoned long ago. *Assistance*, conversely, is tantamount to consulting my personal board of directors. I've selected friends, family members, and colleagues to help me make big decisions, steer me out of muddy waters, and remind me what I value most in my life.

Today my board consists of three sober friends, my sister, my closest colleague, and two trusted business associates—one of whom is currently taking the Somatic Experiencing clinical training. Somatic Experiencing, or SE, is a trauma-focused, body-centered therapeutic model founded by Dr. Peter Levine. *Soma* means "body" in Greek, and the training teaches therapists and healers to assess where a client's unresolved trauma may still be stuck in their body and to heal a nervous system that's stuck in the fight, flight, or freeze response. My friend has been sharing about the case studies she's been working on and gently suggests that my nervous system may need a tune up. Reminding myself to always remain curious about what's underneath the symptoms, I agree. I find a practitioner whom I begin to see twice a week. The experience is incredible. Together we work on releasing energy of past trauma that has been stored in my body, causing me discomfort and blocking my connection to soul.

Just as I am getting relief in my nervous system, my physical symptoms are escalating. I develop a horrible cough and my chest is heavy with each breath. Since I have no fever, my doctor says it's still best to stay home and use the inhaler she has prescribed. Soon I develop a rash all over my upper body, and the tear in my rotator cuff—an injury I've had for two years—becomes excruciatingly painful.

After six months without any relief, I know something is terribly wrong. Not being able to pinpoint the problem becomes increasingly stressful. Once again, Soulbriety saves me. Instead of becoming depressed and defeated, as I might have done a decade earlier, I reach out for more assistance. I call my orthopedic surgeon about my shoulder. Access to elective surgeries is just opening up again after the pandemic peak, so as soon as he hears how much pain I'm in, he insists we book the surgery. I know the recovery from shoulder surgery can be intense and painful and more assistance will be needed, so I have my friend Valerie come stay with me following the procedure. She will cook for me, help me bathe, and—very importantly—manage my painkillers. Regardless of the number of years I have been sober, I know I'm not to be trusted administering my own pills.

A few days after my surgery, Valerie comes into my room and says she smells something funny in the guest room where she's staying. I have rarely gone in the guest room over the past year, as no one has been at my house. The room acts as an extended closet and storage space when I am alone. After a few days of searching the house for the source of the smell, we find what look to be mold spores on the inside of the air conditioning vents. I immediately call to have the house properly inspected. The results of the tests are devastating. *Black mold.* I am told by the experts that I have to leave the premises immediately and I can't take anything with me, as it is all invaded with mold spores. I look at them in disbelief.

"Is this why I am so sick?" I ask.

"Most likely," he says. "You have been breathing in the spores, and they colonize and grow in any environment— including the human body." *What the hell?!*

With my arm immobilized in a brace and sling, I walk out of the house with my two dogs, laptop, phone, and the clothes on my back. The clothes have to be thrown out immediately when I get to my new place. Speaking of which, where am I even going? There is a pandemic happening and hotels are not an option. I start calling my closest friends, including Luke—the one who had held me the day Andy passed away. Turns out he and his wife are out of town and they offer to let me move into their home immediately. Upon my arrival, a bag of new clothes shows up from my friend Jamie. Since the pandemic has shut down travel and I'm working from home, I don't need much—mostly just comfy clothes for the house. My friend Karen picks me up a bunch of toiletries, and I am set for now. I feel my nervous system settle a bit. But the gravity of losing everything is profound. It takes a few days to sink in and I notice I'm starting to feel sorry for myself. *How will I manage? I can't believe I have lost everything I own. My home is completely gone.* But quickly I remember what Soulbriety has taught me about the importance of my belief system. I repeat to myself what I know to be true:

I am the Hero of my Soul Journey.

Soul is my guide.

It's possible to heal from trauma and soul loss.

Dark Nights are essential to gain wisdom.

The Rising is just around the corner.

Reconnecting to soul makes me feel at home.

Soulbriety is the only way to live a meaningful and purposeful life—no matter what.

One by one, the soul-centered relationships I have culti-vated over the years are there for me, shining light when I am surrounded by darkness. My friends walk with me through this scary time, offering their light when my world is in dark-ness. Ten years prior, I can't imagine what this incident would have done to me. But today, my soul friendships catch me when I fall. I relax into their unconditional love, no-questions-asked offers of help, and life-saving humor.

As my nervous system rights itself over the days and weeks that follow, I once again venture into the imaginal for guidance. I call in my trusted parts—Trixie, Gwen, Short Pants, and Flossy—and ask them to speak. I want to make sure all of their voices are part of my recovery from this ill-ness to ensure we're all rowing the boat in the same direction.

As I care for my psyche, I also care for my body. The mold has left me with a chronic inflammatory illness, and recovery requires me to go on a special diet as I try to rid my body of the toxins. I am diligent about following it and making sure that I focus my intention on clearing my insides of any poison that may be lurking in my body. I dive back into nourishing habits, listening to more music, taking walks all around the neighbor-hood, reading books I have been wanting to read for years.

While the losses have been traumatic and the physical symptoms won't heal overnight, I know I've got this. Just as with the recovery from the breakup with Jimmy, I know I can trust soul to get me through. In the meantime, I have my so-briety, I have loving friendships, I have my practice of self-nurturing, and I have the knowledge that even this dark night has something to teach me. All of these elements together make up my plan for Soulbriety—a worldview that guides me and enables me to grow down into myself more and more as each day passes. As I begin to nourish my soul again, I connect back to my inner world. To my surprise, a message is waiting for me there. In spite of my best intentions—to get healthy, grow my business, and take a master class on trauma online—soul has a deeper, more meaningful plan in mind for me. The tiny acorn of my life purpose, which over and over shows me exactly how to grow down into the next version of myself, begins to stir. Soon I hear the call: it's time to start writing the book.

CHAPTER TWELVE

The Hero's Journey

For most of my life I was in search of a savior, a protector, a hero. From an early age I developed a belief that something was wrong with me. That I wasn't safe and I definitely wasn't capable of surviving on my own. No one said this to me in so many words, but life experiences left those Post-it Notes on my soul. Even after I got sober, I still had a skewed belief system. My unhealed trauma had me searching for a fairy-tale Hollywood ending, left me waiting for the prince to come and rescue me. I was getting stronger and more independent in certain ways, but in other ways I was still being run by my past experiences. If I'd broken out the "life balance wheel" I use with clients today, I would have seen that my pie contained one enormous slice of work, plus another smaller slice of unhealthy romantic relationships. But I wasn't practicing Soulbriety then, so I didn't know how to look at my life through the lens of soul. Instead I wore a mask that, because I never took it off, I started to believe *was* me. Even in sobriety, I never paused to let the essence of my true self mature. I was still being driven by a need to "get there," with the "there" being the next validation of my false sense of self. I couldn't separate what had happened to me in the past from my present experience. I was living in a story where the hero was elsewhere, certainly not looking for me, not helping me, not caring about me. So all I could do was wait in pain to be rescued.

The crumbling of the disguise of a relationship I thought I had with Jimmy was the final test, the moment of truth, and, ultimately, the dismantling of the lifelong myth. I was knocked to my knees, but thanks to my Soulbriety training I had the power to heal and I knew it. I knew in my heart there was never anything behind the curtain in Oz; the wizard, the phantom hero, was all a charade. I had to call forth everything I had learned up until that moment. In other words, I had to save myself. All of us hit this truth at some point: no one else is coming. Heroism is an inside job, where the majority of the heavy lifting must be done by you. *I* was the hero of my story, no one else.

My story is not unique. When life is viewed through the lens of soul, each of us has an untold heroism within us. I mentioned earlier that the archives of Joseph Campbell, twentieth-century philosopher and expert in the myths of the world, are housed at Pacifica. The map of the Hero's Journey, which he wrote about in his 1949 book, *The Hero with a Thousand Faces*, reveals how each and every one of us is on a journey to the heart of our own personal myth. One important effect of viewing life through this lens is that dark nights become meaningful, rather than disruptions to be avoided.

We see that they are not optional, but are in fact prerequisites for the soul's maturation. But to see our lives as a meaningful quest where we are the central character, we have to go deeper than is comfortable. It requires us to bring consciousness and willingness to even the hardest moments. We must consent to descending into the underworld and staying with the pain as long as it takes to alchemize our difficult experiences. In other words, we can't expect to feel good all the time. Some amount of suffering is essential to create meaning and purpose in your life. For this reason, not only are dark nights part of every hero's quest since the dawn of time, they are the path to feeling truly safe, alive, awake, and worthy. If you undertake the mission they present to you, you can expect to come out the other side with depth, courage, and wisdom beyond what you ever thought possible for yourself. These are the promises of living your Soulbriety.

The stages of Campbell's Hero's Journey may not unfold for you in exactly the order he mapped out, and that's fine. Each person's life journey is completely unique. That said, it can be useful to study the stages, so you can start to keep an eye out for which lessons and opportunities for growing down are available to you, right now.

Taking the traditional twelve stages as a jumping-off point, here's my interpretation of the turning points you may want to be looking out for:

Stage 1: Your Everyday Life. You are living your life, just going through the motions; unconsciously walking through from one day to the next, not thinking too deeply about anything.

Stage 2: A Whisper from Soul. You hear a whisper, you get an idea, or you have a dream or a desire to rise up that doesn't fit into your life the way it is today. It can also appear if you are feeling unsatisfied, depressed, or directionless. You may start to wonder if there's something more out there for you, asking yourself, "Is this all there is?"

Stage 3: Turning Away. You are too afraid of upsetting the applecart of your life, so you deny the call. You push it away, tune it out, and carry on the same as you always have. You may continue to hear the call in the background, but you ignore it as much as possible.

Stage 4: A Guide Appears. You encounter something—a work of art, a book, or, often, an amazing and encouraging person—and you are suddenly inspired. You can see that others have followed the call and that it worked for them. You see a concrete example of what you're missing by staying stuck in your safe little life. Somewhere deep inside you start to believe maybe you *can* follow your call after all.

Stage 5: Leap of Faith. You courageously proceed to the unknown, crossing some threshold—literal or just symbolic—into a new and unfamiliar world.

Stage 6: Lions and Tigers and Bears! Now in this unfamiliar world you are faced with twists and turns you didn't expect. Speed bumps, dead ends, and brick walls. You feel discouraged. No sooner do you think you need to turn around and "go home" than you experience some small victory. You gain confidence and continue.

Stage 7: At the Threshold. You are so close to the thing you have wanted—you can taste it and smell it, just beyond the gate in front of you. But in despair you realize that, even though you are right there at the door to the gate, you do not have the key to enter.

Stage 8: The Moment of Truth. Here you are face-to-face with your deepest fear. You muster all your strength, courage, and teachings thus far and face combat. This is the epitome of your inner crisis.

Stage 9: Alchemizing. In order to be given the key, you must dig deeper. You have to go inside your inmost cave and be willing to endure the pain of laying down your old beliefs. You become willing to die a spiritual death in order to transform into someone who can continue on the journey.

Stage 10: Enlightenment. Even though you were terrified and never thought you'd make it, you have achieved great things. You've learned what it means to have real courage and have accomplished your initial goal. But you've also developed wisdom enough to know that this might not be the end of the journey.

Stage 11: The Ultimate Challenge. You face a final test, one you didn't see coming. It may take you down to your knees, but you have more power than you know. You must make one final decision: Will you get up off the floor and do the inner work to heal your deepest wounds? And if so, will you be willing to share what you have learned with others in need?

Stage 12: Sharing Your Wisdom. Now home to a new world you have created for yourself, you are the hero others look up to. With you as their inspiring ally, they too gain the courage to set out on their own quest—with the faith that they, too, can return anew.

I'm explaining these stages in images and metaphors because that is the language we speak to do our inner work. Remember, soul likes symbols, myths, and storytelling. As you become more familiar with these stages, you'll start to see how useful these metaphors are. Part of living in your Soulbriety is getting really comfortable with seeing your life as the story of a hero, one whose challenges and obstacles have an important purpose. No longer do you have to face difficult moments and wonder if the despair will go on forever; you know the pain is not a bottomless well, it's just a stage. In fact, it's a useful moment of learning that will make you wiser and happier as you move forward.

So how about taking a moment to really ask yourself which of these stages resonates most with where you are right now. If it's just stage one—what I call "Your Everyday Life"—that's fine. Reading this book may be the first whisper that will take you across the threshold into stage two. My best advice is to try not to refuse your calls forever. The way your soul gets your attention is to increase the level of discomfort until you can't stand it anymore. If you can take the leaps bravely, you won't bypass your dark nights but you may be able to skip over some suffering.

When we make a habit of seeing our current life circumstances as part of our hero's journey, we are reminded that our everyday existence regardless of what is happening—good or bad—has *meaning*. Not just meaning for us, but for everyone we encounter. Each of our painful experiences alchemizes into gold to be shared with other human beings. This is the greatest gift, the most powerful life purpose we could hope for: to be a human being on the journey of life, sharing what we've learned along the way with others. Contrary to the common belief that we're each just floating through life with no real goal or direction, viewing our experience as the path of the hero toward the Holy Grail—whatever that grail is for you— helps us remain humble, patient, and honored to be part of the greater quest.

Sobriety came in stage four of my own journey, and I've been through all the stages dozens of times since. Now, with the soul-whisper telling me it's time to write a book, I see that I'm in stage two again. After so much practice at this, I know that refusing the call will not end the whispers, it will only cause me unnecessary delay. So this time, I just say yes. The more I write, the clearer it becomes that I need to share these stories—not as advice, but to help readers recognize the unknown yet incredibly important messages their own stories hold. I find that the stories of my life no longer feel entirely "mine"—deeply personal and shameful. Instead, they start feeling . . . universal. I realize that my lessons may be helpful to others and that—like any hero's journey—mine needs to culminate with sharing the "healing elixir" I'd found with others. And so this book is born.

SEEING THE WORLD THROUGH SOULBRIETY

So you can see, I believe our journey together was predestined—part of each of our soul maps long before we encountered one another. Perhaps you're in stage three of your journey, and I am a soul guide that has shown up to light your path. Regardless, it is my hope that you will feel inspired by what you've read here to begin—or continue—exploring what Soulbriety means for you. While your story is completely different from mine, there are certain tools I've used that may be useful to you, too. So I'm offering four of them to you, here at the end of my own story, with a bit of instruction to help you integrate them into your own personal Soulbriety plan. Stepping forward onto your soul path can be rocky at times, so think of these tools as supports for your journey. My hope is that they will give you something concrete to come back to when you feel you've lost your way. If you lean on them, I promise they will help you reconnect with that deepest part of you—your very essence.

#1 Tell Your Story

Stories give importance, meaning, and direction to our lives. Humans are the only species that tells stories, and we've been doing it since the dawn of time. Stories inspire us, make us feel included in a larger community, teach us things about ourselves, help us feel compassion for others, solidify traditions, give us strength to cross thresholds, and help us establish meaning where on our own we might just see difficulty. Deeply human questions like, *Why am I here? Has anyone else ever felt this way? Will it get better? What happens now?* and *How will I make it through?* have been answered, over and over throughout time, by stories.

Storytelling is also a pathway to discovering our own soul. Looking back to where it all began is the only way for us to understand where we are, today, on our own journey. We have to tell our stories in order to see our patterns, weaknesses, challenges, achievements, and moments of bravery. For this reason, the first step to living a life of Soulbriety is becoming willing to tell our own story.

So grab your pen and journal, voice-to-text app, video camera, or whatever recording device you like best and start telling your story. Start with "Once upon a time" and let the memories flow from there. Talk like you're speaking to an old friend. Or maybe a new friend, someone you think could benefit from your accumulated wisdom. Begin at the beginning, but don't worry if you find yourself jumping around—this is not a place for self-criticism. If you haven't processed a traumatic experience with a professional, I recommend marking that moment with a headline rather than going deep into the details. Be protective of your brain by not triggering a survival response. You can simply say, "Then a trauma happened," and move on.

Once you've told the story, consider telling it again. You'd be surprised what details you will remember the second time around. Soulbriety isn't a one-and-done program. It's an ongoing process, an excavation that goes layer by layer. Over the course of a life lived by soul, you will tell your story dozens of times, and each time it will be different. This first time through is a foundation you will build on for many years to come.

#2 Live Curiously

As a reminder, soul is your essence, your map, your ally, and your guide. You don't have a soul, you *are* soul. So how do you connect? There are so many ways.

Start with committing to getting curious about your life. It's your job to uncover and discover what the acorn of your soul wants to grow into. It begins with reflection. The aim is to ignite your passion, live in purpose, continue meaning making, and saturate your soul with care and attention.

If you need inspiration to make what is unknown known, I recommend journaling. *What do I need to remember? Who is showing up? What is missing in my life?* One especially potent way to reach parts of yourself that are hidden from your conscious mind is to write with your nondominant hand. This forces you to concentrate more on the process of writing than on *what* you're writing, which allows your subconscious to come through. Your inner world can speak more freely and you can tap into the wisdom you are craving, which is the goal when you're on a soul-discovery mission.

Maybe writing or speaking is not as comfortable for you as drawing, painting, sculpting, or other forms of art. Pick the medium that feels most natural for you. Once you've come to a completion point with your work, notice the colors you used, the shapes and quality of lines, the images you included. Reflect back to what the piece is saying to you—listen carefully.

Music is yet another powerful tool for evoking deep feelings and bringing our attention to memories, allowing us to reflect on parts of ourselves we may have forgotten. Try dancing, taking a quiet walk, or simply closing your eyes and letting your body move to music. I also like to put on songs whose lyrics speak to me and sing along as loudly as I can—whatever works for you.

As you do, try sinking into how you feel; where you are feeling pain in your body, heart, and soul; and what you may need to address in order to alchemize that pain and release it.

Nourish your soul by spending time with relationships that allow you to be yourself—the ones that inspire you, where you feel safe. Try drawing a pie-chart-style balance wheel with slices for family, work, health, relationships, spirituality, and any other areas you care about. Notice which pieces are larger and which are smaller. Consciously fill your schedule with those pieces that are lacking, to bring the different areas of your life into balance. Read books that spark your curiosity or inspire you. Really connect with people you happen to encounter during the day by looking directly into their eyes as you speak with them, as eye contact creates a deeper soul connection. Listen carefully from the heart; the person in front of you may be speaking exactly the words of wisdom you need at this moment. Spend time with the people who make you feel most at home. Set an intention before you go to sleep, asking for soul to be revealed to you in your dreams. Then, if you remember an image from your dreams—a figure, animal, symbol, or storyline—write it down. You don't need to try and interpret the meaning, for these are autonomous figures. Simply ask, why are you here? *What might my soul be communicating with this image? What does it remind me of? Where in my life might I need a message like this one?* Take some time to really meditate on this piece of information your soul has provided. Similarly, take the time to meditate on any symptoms you're experiencing, whether physical or emotional. Get curious about why they might be showing up in your life right now. Don't worry if you don't get answers; all will be revealed at just the right time. You cannot rush your psyche, but if you let her know you are listening, she will eventually speak to you.

Go back to your acorn, and check in on how closely you're following its map in your life. Start by remembering who you were as a kid. Children don't yet have the buildup of Post-it Notes that tell them they can't be who and what they want. They just know what they like and what they don't like. What did you love to do as a child? When you were eight and nine and ten years old, what were your passions? Your curiosities? What activities could you get lost in for hours? The answers to these questions are like clues on a treasure hunt, and the treasure is your true purpose.

Now, think about your interests today. If you could have dinner with anyone in the world, who would it be? If you could go back to school, what would you want to learn? If you could live any lifestyle, what would it be like? Take some time to write about the younger you and the you today. Where do their interests overlap? How might you give the acorn more space to expand in your day-to-day life? Set some intentions. Small changes will get you a long way, so don't try to make a full-life pivot all at once. Take your time, feel your way, and listen to your soul's whispers.

#3 Enter the Imaginal

If there's one soul process I want you to lean into, it's developing a relationship with your imaginal. As I said earlier, your imaginal is where your imagination meets soul. It serves as a gateway for connecting with the personas, images, symbols, and archetypes that are within us. Consciously entering this realm as a practice, getting to know it, and creating a welcoming space within gives you a safe, warm home you can retreat into for processing and healing. It's a place where you can reconnect with lost parts of yourself, dialoguing with them to help mend any soul fragmentation that may have happened throughout your soul journey.

One imaginal location I have shared with you is my "inmost cave." My cave is a place in which I can find comfort during a dark night; it's where I alchemize difficult experiences into wisdom. But I also enter when things are going well, to prepare the space for those inevitable moments when I'll be forced there by events beyond my control.

In preparation for my active imagination session, I dim the lights in the room, light a candle, and turn on some soft music. This ritual helps me create a safe space for the unknown to enter. (It also allows me to mark a distinct completion to the process by blowing out the candle and turning the lights back on when I'm done.) Then I close my eyes and, in my mind, descend down the staircase into the cave. Once there I may simply sit with my feelings and watch them alchemize or I may invite my soul to present me with an image or persona needing my attention. As I've already mentioned, the personas

I meet with most often are Trixie, Gwen, Flossy, and Short Pants. I don't meet them in the cave, which is my own private space. Instead, in my imaginal, these four parts of me live together in an old VW van—the kind you might find parked outside a Grateful Dead concert. If I need them, I ask that they pull over the van to the side of the road for a meeting.

Once we've created a relationship to our inner world, we become more sensitive to what it's telling us. For example, we may start to feel vaguely "out of sorts," "edgy," or "not ourselves," but we might not know the source. When we can't pinpoint an issue, instead we can describe it in the form of an image or persona. Intuitively, what does the feeling look like? If it had a shape, would it be a person, animal, or other object? If it had a color, what would it be? Over the course of time, we may see this part come back to visit often. If so, it's a good idea to give it a name.

Once we're familiar with it, we can write down this part's characteristics, their sense of style, what they sound like, how they get our attention, and their core beliefs. In time, we start to recognize when they're asking for our attention, and we look forward to dialoguing with them because their wisdom is useful to us. If you're having a hard time putting an image to a particular part, there's a beautiful exercise I love. Get out an unlined piece of paper and a pencil and sit down in front of a mirror. Without being self-critical or perfectionistic, draw a self-portrait. When you are done you will see an image that *is* you but looks nothing like you: you're meeting one of your parts. Spend time with the picture, leaving it out where you can see it, and eventually it will speak to you. Wait patiently without forcing the process.

If you've never done active imagination before and would like support, you can find guided meditations on my website www.drhallerman.com under the tab *Soulbriety Meditations.*

#4 Acknowledge Your Dark Nights

Soul loss is inevitable; we all experience it. Sometimes it's obvious, and other times it is subtle. But if you find yourself feeling depressed, anxious, or like you're swimming in darkness, you're likely bumping up against a dark night of the soul. Take a minute to pause and reflect. Have you experienced an injury, either to your body or soul? Are you brokenhearted over a breakup or grieving after a loss? Has your life changed quickly and drastically, leaving you feeling confused, overwhelmed, alone, and frozen? If so, you may be coming face-to-face with soul loss.

You cannot go around this kind of dark night; there is no way out except to stay with it. Imagine yourself as the alchemist and the darkness as raw material that might be turned to gold, given the right circumstances. Instead of letting it envelop you, you can place this material in a glass beaker and heat it up. As it gets hotter and hotter, it changes into something new, something whose help you've needed in your life. This is where patience is essential. You are experiencing a metamorphosis, and you cannot speed up the process. You can only allow your pain to break you apart and rebuild you slowly as a wiser, more powerful you. As long as you don't run away from the discomfort, transformation *will* happen and you will be its beneficiary. Your grief may propel you to be of service to others in a similar situation. . . . your job loss or financial struggle may leave you no choice but to try a career path that will turn out to be more fulfilling . . . your breakup may reveal painful relationship patterns you'd been unwilling to examine but are now ready to let go.

⸻

EVERYTHING I AM today stems from my decision to get sober all those years ago. My sobriety gave me the opportunity to have a life; I had been practicing *dying* every single day before that. Once I made a decision to get and stay sober I began to *live*. What I didn't yet know how to do was to live wholeheartedly, courageously, and honestly. The trauma kept me sick, even in sobriety. But my life became worthy of meaning when I focused on soul. I followed its guidance—sometimes reluctantly—and in spite of countless mistakes and moments of suffering, I kept going. I knew each stage of my journey had a purpose and that the meaning of life could only be found in staying present to its unfolding. As I read back through this book, I am forced to acknowledge the pain, fear, immaturity, selfishness, and ego that have been part of my process. I am far from perfect. But I also know that I am strong, resilient, and the only hero my story will ever have. What's more, I love who I've become thanks to each of the turning points I've survived. I am so proud of the Recovery Management Agency, my colleagues there, and our mission to make the world of addiction and mental health easier to understand and navigate. Every day we are answering the questions, *Do you think there is any hope? Can I get better? Can my loved one survive this? Will they ever have a normal life?* To the last question, I can only smile. Adversity, suffering, and grief are part of life. Without recognizing the inevitable darkness, we cannot fully reach our potential. So for me "normal" is defined as *not being afraid of the dark*. Being able to sit in it, learn from it, and focus on what it's trying to teach you. Writing this book has been an adventure like no other for me. I traveled dangerous roads, found my way out of quicksand many times over, braved the tumultuous waters of my emotions, and faced my most terrifying demons. Yet I continued. I knew it was a soul calling to write this book, so that others could take refuge in my story. But I now see that it was important for me, as well. Today, looking back at my life, I am inspired by what I have accomplished. My inner light will flicker again at some point, threatening to go out. But in living from a place of purpose, I know my soul will guide me through. I can only hope this book inspires the same awareness in you.

Here in my last few weeks of writing, my mom is once again staying with me in LA. Each night I read her chapters, and we laugh and cry together. One night she turns to me.

"I'm starting to realize that I was not the mom I thought I was," she says.

"You've been on your own soul journey, Mom," I say. "And it's not over yet."

I see it sink in, and something changes in that moment. Soulbriety is the work of a lifetime. I see a light go on inside of her as she contemplates how far she has come and the meaning that lies down the road ahead. She is seeing herself, in this moment, as the hero of her own story.

May it be so for all of us.

Resources

ADDICTION AND RECOVERY

Alcoholics Anonymous is a resource for those who are suffering
with alcohol, drug abuse, or other addictions. More information
can be found at www.aa.org and in the following books:

> *The Book That Started It All: The Original Working
> Manuscript of Alcoholics Anonymous*
>
> *Alcoholics Anonymous: The Big Book*
>
> *The Twelve Steps and Twelve Traditions*

Al-Anon is a twelve-step group for loved ones whose lives have
been affected by the disease of addiction or alcoholism. More information is available at www.al-anon.org or in these books:

> *How Al-Anon Works for Families & Friends of Alcoholics*
>
> *Al-Anon's Twelve Steps & Twelve Traditions*
>
> *Paths to Recovery: Al-Anon's Steps, Traditions, and Concepts*
>
> *Courage to Change: One Day at a Time in Al-Anon II*

Other useful addiction and recovery websites include:

Recovery 2.0: r20.com

Generation S.O.S: www.generationsos.org

BOOKS

Codependency is an emotional and behavioral condition that affects an individual's ability to set proper boundaries and have healthy relationships. It often coexists with addiction. For more information, see these books:

Codependent No More: How to Stop Controlling Others and Start Caring for Yourself by Melody Beattie

The Language of Letting Go by Melody Beattie

Facing Codependence: What It Is, Where It Comes from, How It Sabotages Our Lives by Pia Mellody

Some of the best books on trauma healing, by leaders in the field, include:

In an Unspoken Voice: How the Body Releases Trauma and Restores Goodness by Peter Levine

Waking the Tiger: Healing Trauma by Peter Levine

The Body Keeps the Score: Brain, Mind, and Body in the Healing of Trauma by Bessel Van Der Kolk

In the Realm of Hungry Ghosts: Close Encounters with Addiction by Gabor Maté

What Happened to You? Conversations on Trauma, Resilience and Healing by Bruce D. Perry and Oprah Winfrey

Healing the Traumatized Self: Consciousness, Neuroscience, Treatment by Paul Frewen and Ruth Lanius

RESOURCES

For more understanding about the brain and the mind:

Brainstorm: The Power and Purpose of the Teenage Brain by Daniel J. Siegel

The Developing Mind: How Relationships and the Brain Interact to Shape Who We Are by Daniel J. Siegel

Mindsight: The New Science of Personal Transformation by Daniel J. Siegel

If you are interested in learning more about the Hero's Journey, I recommend:

The Hero with a Thousand Faces by Joseph Campbell

The Hero's Journey: Joseph Campbell on His Life and Work by Joseph Campbell

For more about vulnerability, shame, and empathy, I cannot recommend Brené Brown more highly. All of her books are wonderful, but my favorites are:

The Gifts of Imperfection: Let Go of Who You Think You're Supposed to Be and Embrace Who You Are by Brené Brown

Atlas of the Heart: Mapping Meaningful Connection and the Language of Human Experience by Brené Brown

I find that my clients and I easily identify with the "hero's journey" at the heart of Glennon Doyle's books:

Love Warrior: A Memoir by Glennon Doyle

Untamed by Glennon Doyle

For more on depth psychology and archetypal psychology:

Re-Visioning Psychology by James Hillman

RESOURCES

The Soul's Code: In Search of Character and Calling by James Hillman

Archetypal Psychology by James Hillman

Memories, Dreams, Reflections by C. G. Jung

Modern Man in Search of a Soul by C. G. Jung

Jung on Active Imagination by C. G. Jung

Dancing in the Flames: The Dark Goddess in the Transformation of Consciousness by Marion Woodman and Elinor Dickson

Henry Corbin first named the "imaginal," distinguishing the imaginal realm from the imaginary.

Mundus Imaginalis: Or, The Imaginary and the Imaginal by Henry Corbin

Wisdom of the Psyche: Depth Psychology After Neuroscience by Ginette Paris

Thomas Moore's books gave me the introduction to understanding soul. He was on my dissertation committee at Pacifica and gave me both the confidence to continue writing on the important topic of soul and addiction and the hard lesson about not cutting corners in my writing and taking the time to let psyche help the process.

Dark Nights of the Soul: A Guide to Finding Your Way Through Life's Ordeals by Thomas Moore

Care of the Soul: A Guide for Cultivating Depth and Sacredness in Everyday Life by Thomas Moore

Here are the books I most often find myself giving to clients, on the subjects of parenting, psychology, and personal growth:

Cutting: Understanding and Overcoming Self-Mutilation by
Steven Levenkron

*Stop Walking on Eggshells: Taking Your Life Back When
Someone You Care About Has Borderline Personality
Disorder* by Paul T. Mason and Randi Kreger

*The Road Less Traveled: A New Psychology of Love,
Traditional Values, and Spiritual Growth* by M. Scott Peck

Man's Search for Meaning by Viktor Frankl

*The Teenage Brain: A Neuroscientist's Guide to Raising
Adolescents and Young Adults* by Frances E. Jensen

*The Feeling of What Happens: Body and Emotion in the
Making of Consciousness* by Antonio Damasio

OTHER RESOURCES

David Kessler is one of my favorite experts working with
grief. His resources can be found at www.grief.com

To take the Adverse Childhood Experiences Study quiz,
visit www.acestoohigh.com/got-your-ace-score

If you're interested in the schools I've attended and
certificate programs I have taken, visit:

Pacifica Graduate Institute, www.pacifica.edu

UCLA Drug and Alcohol Counseling Certificate,
www.uclaextension.edu

Soul Psychology with Thomas Moore,
www.thomasmooresoul.com

NICABM, www.nicabm.com

Acknowledgments

Writing a book is one of the most soul-connected experiences I have ever had. My memories, personal narrative, and soul are uniquely mine. Yet, none of our stories are entirely personal, and those involved have their own perspectives on the experiences we've shared. So I first want to acknowledge my family and express my extreme gratitude for their willingness for me to share our personal moments in this book. My family's support has been, throughout my lifetime, one of my greatest teachers and greatest strengths.

Today I am close with both of my parents. We can all sit down to Thanksgiving dinner or even take vacations together, which says a lot about how much all of us have grown over the years. Big thanks to Mom and Dad for letting me be me in my storytelling.

To my sister, whom I love with all my heart and soul: I will always be thankful for you. It's been the gift of a lifetime that I get to walk this earth with you by my side. Thank you for all of it!

To Sammy and Charley: Thank you for letting me participate in your lives to the fullest. I could not love two people on the planet more than I love you!

To Goose and Gus Gus, who probably won't read this but deserve to be acknowledged for all their unconditional love, companionship, and gentle reminders when it was time to take a mental health break and go outside for a walk.

To my agent and main squeeze Margaret King, who believed in me when I emailed her and asked her if she would possibly read my proposal. Margaret, your belief in me and Soulbriety, from day one, has meant the world to me. You have made my dream come true, and I will be forever grateful to have you by my side. Thank you for indulging me when I wanted to play the role of agent—you are far better at it than I am now!

To Ari and Mark: Thank you for the constant support of my business, dreams, and creative work. Having the two of you in my corner all of these years means everything.

To Lauren Marino: From the moment we spoke about the proposal I knew I wanted you to be my editor. Thank you for choosing me, believing in me, and walking me through this process. And big gratitude to the amazing team at Hachette: Cisca Schreefel, Martha Whitt, Mary Tederstrom, Emily Epstein White, Monica Oluwek, Linda Mark, Amanda Kain, Sara Pinsonault, Michelle Aielli, Michael Barrs, Lauren Rosenthal, and Mary Ann Naples.

Thank you, Sarah Hall and Kristyn White, for your tireless work in getting the word out about *Soulbriety*—and getting it into the hands of those that need it most.

To my RMA team: Allison, Chris, Mike, Sherry, Lulu, and Dara, you have each supported me in endless ways over the years of dissertation-, proposal-, and then manuscript-writing. Allison, you have allowed me the space to write and be creative, and you've generously listened whenever I got excited about a paragraph and had to read it to someone. I love you all and am endlessly proud of your contributions to—and continued partnerships in—the important work we do.

To Wendy, Dre, Steph, Jamie, and Joy: You were my family by choice from the day we met. We've grown up together, walked through the highlights of our lifetimes together, and have helped each other through many a dark night. Thank you for always being there for me. Always.

To my two sober soul-sisters, Zoe and Gabby: Thank you for walking this road of happy destiny with me, for always inspiring me to do more and be more to others, and for reminding me about my moral compass in my times of need.

To two very special sober ladies, Cynthia and Jamie: Thank you from the bottom of my heart for leading the way and walking me through some of the toughest moments of my life. Thank you for helping me to save my life.

Lastly, thank you to Kelly Notaras and her entire team at KN Literary. There would be no book—certainly not one that reads this way—without you! You have taught me how to be a writer. Our relationship started with you as my editor and writing coach. Over the past two years, you've also been my therapist, English teacher, and close confidante. You told me the truth, challenged me, and stretched me out of my comfort zone. I am forever grateful to have gone through this soul journey with you—and to have met a friend for life!